Let Us Remember

Remember

STORIES *of the* HOLY PRESENCE OF GOD

Brother George Van Grieken, FSC, Editor

saint mary's press

Christian Brothers Conference

Design and production by Saint Mary's Press (www.smp.org).

Cover image: We thank the Dutch artist Ad Arma for giving permission to use one of his works for the front cover of the book. (www.adarma-art.com/en)

Back cover quotation: Johnston, John, FSC. "The Pastoral Letters (1986–2000)" Lasallian Resource Center, Napa, CA, 2016: 498.

Quotation at conclusion of Prefix: De La Salle, John Baptist. *Explanation of the Method of Interior Prayer.* Translated by Richard Arnandez. Edited by Donald Mouton. Landover, MD: Lasallian Publications, 1995: 59.

Quotations from Meditations *by St. John Baptist de La Salle contained herein are from the following:* De La Salle, John Baptist. *Meditations.* Translated by Richard Arnandez, FSC, and Augustine Loes, FSC. Edited by Augustine Loes, FSC, and Francis Huether, FSC. Romeoville, IL: Christian Brothers Conference, 1994.

Names used in this book are pseudonyms unless the person has given explicit permission to use his/her name, or if the person is deceased.

Printed in the United States of America

9202

978-1-59982-988-3

Library of Congress Cataloging-in-Publication Data:
Names: Van Grieken, George, editor.
Title: Let us remember : stories of the holy presence of God / Brother George
    Van Grieken, FSC, editor.
Description: Winona : Saint Mary's Press, 2018.
Identifiers: LCCN 2018016891| ISBN 9781599829883 | ISBN 9781599829890 (e-book)
Subjects: LCSH: Christian Brothers—Education. | Christian education. | God
    (Christianity) | La Salle, Jean Baptiste de, Saint, 1651–1719.
Classification: LCC LC495.C47 L48 2018 | DDC 371.071/2—dc23
LC record available at *https://lccn.loc.gov/2018016891*

Contents

Preface

God is unfailingly present—simply, immeasurably, and always—and we dwell within the limitless borders and opportunities of that presence. A Brother recently told me, as he was reading the morning newspaper, bathed in the warming sun streaming through the window, "You know, Mexican mothers take their babies and early in the morning place them in the sunlight, calling this 'The poor man's blanket.'" The simplicity of the sun's warmth is present for all to appreciate—simply, immeasurably, and always. Its universal impact on so many levels and for so many people, poor and rich alike, is a good analogy for how we might think of God's presence as encountered and described among us, whatever our personal details or circumstances.

Of course, God's reach lies much beyond that of the sun. "*Vocatus atque non vocatus Deus aderit*" ("Bidden or unbidden, God is always present") says a line from Erasmus, carved into the lintel of Carl Jung's house in Switzerland. God's reach goes to the heart of existence and, in the words of Abraham Joshua Heschel, the "true meaning of existence is disclosed in moments of living in the presence of God." Such moments are illustrated by the stories in this book. Their wide spectrum, in both likely and unlikely places, attests to God's unbound presence with us and within us. These are snapshots of God, as it were, touching our hearts, regularly and invariably impacting our lives in ways that are simply profound or profoundly simple, surprisingly unique or amazingly ordinary, via interior insights and dynamics or exterior circumstances and people, in the burning bush or in the whisper of the wind. God's presence is never the same and yet always the same. "Blessed are the pure of heart, for they shall see God." (Mt 5:8)

The stories in this book are about God's manifest presence in the lives of those who share the ministry of education that has been and continues to be informed, shaped, and guided by the spirituality of Saint John Baptist de La Salle (1651–1719), who is the Patron Saint of All Teachers of Youth, the founder of the De La Salle Christian Brothers (Institute of the Brothers of the Christian Schools), and the charismatic touchstone for all those who live and work within Lasallian ministries. It is a book of stories where God's presence speaks through the here and now, where God is seen to dwell within people's lives. All stories give shape, substance, hope, example, and inspiration that lasts, as exemplified by the stories of Scripture. In this volume, you are invited to recognize God's handiwork in the lives of those engaged in Lasallian ministries and perhaps attend to similar previously unrecognized instances of God's presence in your own life, your own story. De La Salle calls all of his followers to be genuine "ambassadors of Jesus Christ," who is God's ultimate presence for, in, and through us. These stories are snapshots of that invitation and reality.

Brother Robert Schieler, FSC, Superior General, wrote in his 2017 Pastoral Letter, "Our stories are really important. They are the glue that holds us together. Our stories carry our memories and memories are conveyors of grace." The stories in this volume convey the grace of encountering the presence of God among the daily details of Lasallian life, reflecting different ways of understanding what is meant by the presence of God. There are also a few contributions that may not relate a specific instance of such an encounter but rather give us a thoughtful reflection about the presence of God. Several offer profound theological ideas of what the presence of God means for us today. Most hold up unique experiential moments when God has graced us with an opportunity of encounter, often during the course of our regular ministry. As such, they are indeed a kind of glue that binds us to one another and to our common Lasallian mission.

The observation of Brother John Crawford, FSC, one of the editors of this volume, about the variety of these stories is worth sharing. "Sometimes these experiences have occurred in natural phenomena, but more often these blessed moments have happened on the holy ground where we Lasallians labor, in classrooms and offices and during the daily performance of our duties. Sometimes, the awareness of God present to us overwhelms us in an instant. On other occasions, we experience God's presence over an expanse of time and through multiple daily interactions. No matter how God has been encountered, each of the essayists in this volume has attempted to capture in our always incomplete words some sense of God ever present."

Prayer, God's presence, and personal experience coalesce in these stories and are shaped into eloquent realities that defy easy distinction. Perhaps this is to be expected whenever there are genuine encounters with or within God's presence. It makes it all the more significant that the contributors to this volume took the time and effort involved in putting their experience on paper. There is always a risk that what is described might be misunderstood or not fully appreciated. For each of the writers, the profound impact of their experience not only overcame their caution in being willing to share it, but the story itself also compelled them to share it with others, as all good stories do. Different writing styles or emphases or expressions may be used by different writers, but these give character to the stories rather than detract from their validity.

Each story also carries an element of enthusiasm that has the impact of a five-year-old running into the house, just bursting with eagerness to share what was seen or experienced. Listening to the story, or reading such stories in the case of this book, will gladden our hearts and stir in us the desire to pursue the same. This is the kind of enthusiasm that De La Salle tells us God has for us, whether in the schools ("Let us remember that we are in the holy presence of God"), in the students ("Recognize Jesus beneath the poor rags of the children"), in prayer ("How happy I am, O my God, to find you always present"), or in anything else ("We know God by faith, and charity makes us love him"). We are privileged to be able to witness some of the ways that such enthusiasm is experienced and lived in the Lasallian world today.

Thanks go to the Publications Committee of the Lasallian Region of North America, where the idea of this book took form, and especially to the editorial committee—Brother Timothy Coldwell, FSC; Brother John Crawford, FSC; Denis de Villers; Elizabeth Moors Jodice (who provided significant support, coordination, and oversight); Marianne Stich, AFSC; and Brother George Van Grieken, FSC. The 131 submitted stories were individually assessed for a variety of qualities according to a standard rubric, with the results compiled for subsequent discussion and consideration. A series of meetings determined a final list of 52 stories, one for each week of the year. Thanks also to Brother Donald Mouton, FSC, and Brother Leonard Marsh, FSC, for translating stories submitted in French and Spanish, and to Saint Mary's Press for editorial assistance, design, layout, and production of the book.

Our very special thanks to all those who shared their stories. God's story with us is never finished, and one book of collected stories is never as important as each individual person's story in God's presence. May this collection of stories help you continue to write your own.

"This I believe, O my God,
that wherever I go I will find you,
and that there is no place not honored by your presence."

—Saint John Baptist de La Salle
(Explanation to the Method of Interior Prayer)

Brother George Van Grieken, FSC
May 15, 2018
Solemnity of Saint John Baptist de La Salle

Introduction

The Holy Presence of God in De La Salle's Spirituality

Saint John Baptist de La Salle had an abiding interest in fostering the remembrance of the holy presence of God, both for himself, the Brothers, and the students in the schools. It is an ongoing and recurring theme in many of his writings and a deep current of his personal spiritual life. His fond desire was to deepen the spiritual lives of his followers and of the students who attended his schools, so that they might come to realize God's intimate involvement in their lives, the one who "guides all things with wisdom and serenity . . . in an imperceptible way and over a long period of time."[1] This engaged "holy presence of God" was a major component of De La Salle's spiritual DNA. Both during De La Salle's time and today, the remembrance or recollection of that presence is central to Lasallian prayer and ministry, because awareness of this presence in the heart and mind fuels our work, empowers our ministry. It guides our personal and community discernment, and sustains our growth in the love of God and one another. It integrates the chapters of our life narrative. Therefore, to look at some specific examples of the wide and deep reach of that phrase in our foundational documents is surely beneficial.

In the 1718 *Rule of the Brothers of the Christian Schools,*[2] De La Salle identifies the presence of God as one of the four "interior supports" of the Institute, holding it among those qualities that are "essential."[3] In the *Collection of Short Treatises,*[4] it is part

---

1 Blain, Jean-Baptiste. *The Life of John Baptist de La Salle, Founder of the Brothers of the Christian Schools.* Translated by Richard Arnandez, FSC. Romeoville, IL: Christian Brothers Conference, 1983. Vol. 1, Bk. 1, 60–61.
2 De La Salle, John Baptist. *Rule and Foundational Documents.* Translated and edited by Augustine Loes, FSC, and Ronald Isetti. Landover, MD: Christian Brothers Conference, 1989.
3 Ibid., 69.
4 De La Salle, John Baptist. *Collection of Various Short Treatises.* Translated by W.J. Battersby, FSC. Edited by Daniel Burke, FSC. Romeoville, IL: Christian Brothers Conference, 1993.

of a list of "Ten Commandments" of the Institute—originally rendered in French verse for ease of recollection: "God ever present you'll adore, and oft his grace and aid implore."[5] In that same *Collection,* which was an abbreviated compilation of various sayings, devotions, practices, and some of his other writings, the importance of remembering "the presence of God" appears in many different contexts.

- *List of Topics for Self-Examination:* "Are you attentive to the holy presence of God?"[6]
- *The Spirit of This Institute:* "They will pay as much attention as they can to the holy presence of God and take care to renew this from time to time."[7]
- *Explanation of the Spirit of Our Institute:* "What is meant by keeping our attention fixed on God? It is to think of the presence of God."[8]
- *Means to Become Interior:* "We must practice recollection . . . because it disposes and assists us to apply ourselves to the presence of God and interior prayer, and gives us facility in doing so."[9]
- *The Divine Office:* "When you recite the Divine Office . . . apply yourself as much as you can to the meaning of the words, to the mysteries alluded to therein, or simply to the presence of God."[10]
- *Holy Mass:* "Frequently recall the thought of the holy presence of God and the respect that the angels have before the divine Majesty."[11]
- *Spiritual Reading:* "Do not begin reading without placing yourself in the presence of God and asking him by a short

5 Ibid., 70.
6 Ibid., 16.
7 Ibid., 31.
8 Ibid., 34.
9 Ibid., 52.
10 Ibid., 56.
11 Ibid., 57.

prayer for the grace and the light to understand and to practice what you will read."[12]

- *Recreation:* "Do not go to recreation too eagerly or with too much effusiveness. Be careful not to become dissipated, and do not lose sight of the presence of God."[13]

Less formally, De La Salle often included recommendations to attend to the presence of God in his letters to the Brothers. These instances highlight the close integration of faith and zeal that constituted the substance and the spirit of the Institute. It is in and through attending to the presence of God—in the chapel and in the classroom—that the Lasallian charism comes to life.

- "The presence of God will be a great advantage to you to help and to inspire you to do your actions well."[14]

- "Applying ourselves to the presence of God is a most useful practice; be faithful to it."[15]

- "To renew and to strengthen your awareness of God's presence, often focus on your inner self. The more you try to achieve this, the easier you will find it to perform your actions and to carry out your duties well."[16]

- "Apply yourself often to remember the presence of God, my very dear Brother. Look upon this practice as your greatest happiness."[17]

- "[M]ake sure that God's holy presence is often with you, for it is the principal fruit of interior prayer."[18]

12 Ibid., 61.
13 Ibid., 63.
14 De La Salle, John Baptist. *The Letters of John Baptist de La Salle.* Translation, introduction, and commentary by Colman Molloy, FSC. Edited with additional commentary by Augustine Loes, FSC. Landover, MD: Lasallian Publications, 1988, reprinted 2007: 20.
15 Ibid., 25.
16 Ibid., 194.
17 Ibid., 210.
18 Ibid., 22.

Attending to the presence of God was also a pervasive invitation for students in the schools. The classic educational work, *The Conduct of Schools*,[19] integrates the recollection of God's presence within the school's daily life—how one enters the classroom, as part of the curriculum, and as occasional reminders during the course of the day.

- "They will be inspired to enter the classroom with profound respect, out of consideration for the presence of God. When they have reached the center of the room, they will make a low bow before the crucifix and will bow to the teacher if one is present."[20]
- "Those who are studying the chart of syllables will learn and repeat the acts of the presence of God."[21]
- "At each hour of the day, some short prayers will be said. These will help the teachers to recollect themselves and recall the presence of God; it will serve to accustom the students to think of God from time to time and to offer God all their actions, and to draw upon themselves God's blessing."[22]

The hourly school prayer, along with all the other prayers stipulated in *Exercises of Piety for the Christian School*,[23] begins with the sign of the cross and is immediately followed by "Let us remember that we are in the holy presence of God." This distinctly Lasallian invitation is as ubiquitous among these prayers as the sign of the cross, and is unfailingly included.

19 De La Salle, John Baptist. *Conduct of Christian Schools*. Translated by F. de La Fontainerie and Richard Arnandez, FSC. Edited by William Mann, FSC. Landover, MD: Lasallian Publications, 1996. This work, based on 40 years of experience and collaboration, was first printed in 1720 and became a foundational influence for many other teaching orders founded in the subsequent centuries. The work was revised and reprinted through 24 editions until the early 1900s.
20 Ibid., 49.
21 Ibid., 55.
22 Ibid., 92.
23 De La Salle, John Baptist. *Religious Instructions and Exercises of Piety for the Christian Schools*. Translated by Richard Arnandez, FSC. Edited by Eugene Lappin, FSC. Landover, MD: Lasallian Publications, 2002.

Even in his book on politeness, *The Rules of Christian Decorum and Civility*,[24] written for young inner-city boys who had little notion of how to behave in polite society, the motivation for proper behavior is directly related to God's presence. De La Salle writes,

- "It is surprising that most Christians look upon decorum and politeness as merely human and worldly qualities and do not think of raising their minds to any higher views by considering them as virtues that have reference to God, to their neighbor, and to themselves."[25]
- "When they [parents and teachers] wish to train children in practices pertaining to bodily care and simple modesty, they should carefully lead them to be motivated by the presence of God. . . . Children should do these things out of respect for God in whose presence they are."[26]

The Method of Interior Prayer

It is in De La Salle's *Explanation of the Method of Interior Prayer*[27] (*Explanation*) that these various dimensions of his spirituality are put together in a way that both shows the outlines of his spirituality and exemplifies the difficulty of expounding it with complete clarity. His perceptible framework for genuine interior prayer—the ongoing existential, interior relationship with God (Father, Son, and Holy Spirit) that constituted his deepest and dearest pursuit and desire—defies easy unpacking. Some have found his method for interior prayer too detailed and labori-

---

24 De La Salle, John Baptist. *The Rules of Christian Decorum and Civility.* Translated by Richard Arnandez, FSC. Edited by Gregory Wright, FSC. Romeoville, IL: Lasallian Publications, 1990. This work was a book that students read after having learned how to read well, so that they might profit by the contents as well as their reading practice. A sample chapter heading reads: "Yawning, Spitting, and Coughing." The earliest copy dates from 1695, and the earliest printed edition was in 1703. There were 150 editions of the book that were published into the twentieth century, and some quotations from the work still show up in modern books on politeness.
25 Ibid., 3.
26 Ibid., 3–4.
27 De La Salle, John Baptist. *Explanation of the Method of Interior Prayer.* Translated by Richard Arnandez, FSC, and Donald Mouton, FSC. Edited by Donald Mouton, FSC. Landover, MD: Christian Brothers Conference, 1995. Much of the substance of this section is more fully developed in the introduction to the *Explanation,* from which it comes.

ous—with its austere style, three dynamic movements, 21 acts, and sentiments more at home in the seventeenth century than the twenty-first. Others have found the primary direction and inner dynamism of his guidance, along with wonderful reflection gems that are dropped along the way, personally appealing, revelatory, and full of insight. When considering this work, it is important to remember that what counts for De La Salle are not the acts but rather the developed disposition of allowing oneself to be filled with God through an interior unity brought about by the action of the Holy Spirit.[28]

The *Explanation* is a book for beginners in the practice of interior prayer, put together after De La Salle's death and based on his talks, conferences, notes, and other resources, especially and including those Brothers who had known him well. When he "retired" at St. Yon in Rouen toward the end of his life, De La Salle spent much of his time guiding the young Brothers in the practice of interior prayer, inspiring, instructing, correcting, and training them in what he believed to be a most essential dimension of their vocation. It was something that he was uniquely able to promote at that time. In terms of its spirit and fundamental content, the *Explanation* was "the last book" that he wrote. It reflects the fruit of his personal experience of interior prayer, his Scripture-based spirituality, his theological training, his years of reflection and practical decisions in founding the Institute, and all of the pieces of his life that had led him to this point. The book was published in 1739, 20 years after his death.

When reading the *Explanation,* the complex yet essentially simple nature of interior prayer emerges as if one were zooming out on Google Earth from a single house to the view of Earth from space: the details are part of something much, much larger and more universal. The elements of this prayer form—explanations, reflections, steps to follow, cautions against scrupulosity,

---

28 Ibid., Introduction, 5.

invitations, and examples for personalizing one's acts of faith—are all pieces of something that is greater than the sum of the parts. Notions about prayer, faith, and God's presence revolve around one another like the color tiles on a Rubik's cube. Yet at the same time, the substance of the book comes across as a work of art, or rather an artist describing a work of art, whereby what is verbally woven slowly emerges into particles of personal perception, brought about by means of cumulatively added layers and nuances, growing relationships and associative connections.

What is very evident, however, is that interior prayer becomes most clearly defined through the settled context that only consistent practice achieves. This requires time. The dancer Martha Graham once said that it took 10 years of hard work in order to become a dancer. "It took years to become spontaneous and simple. Nijinsky took thousands of leaps before the memorable one."[29] Similarly, each intentional pursuit of genuine interior prayer does not arrive fully formed simply through intentionality. It must be willed and practiced over time. The dance of prayer is based on "hard work." It takes shape and grows with the deliberate, patient speed of life itself.

Brother Donald Mouton, FSC, in his excellent introduction to the *Explanation,* writes that "in the mind of De La Salle, prayer that is truly interior escapes all methods. The ultimate consequence of the method is to dispense with the method. This is De La Salle's final recommendation. In prayer, we must allow ourselves to be interiorly and gently drawn by God, even if it is to some sentiment we had not proposed to ourselves beforehand."[30] The goal of De La Salle's method is the formation of a deep interiority in one's soul so as to allow the Holy Spirit to pray in us.

It is eminently worthwhile to examine some of the method's infrastructure in order to enhance our understanding of, and progress towards, this deep interiority.

29 Fox, Matthew. *Creativity.* New York, NY: Penguin Random House, 2002: 170.
30 De La Salle, John Baptist. *Explanation of the Method of Interior Prayer.* Op. cit. Introduction, 12.

There are three movements or stages that constitute the dynamics of De La Salle's interior prayer method.[31]

1. *Recollection into the Presence of God:* distancing ourselves from external preoccupations and moving towards the "depths of our heart," where we encounter the living God at the heart of our lives, and enter into the climate of interior prayer.

2. *A Mystery, Virtue, or Teaching:* engaging in interior prayer's principal activity, which is to fill one's soul with God in and through Jesus Christ; to contemplate the person of Jesus Christ, by focusing on one of his mysteries, virtues, or teachings that may be engaged and brought into one's life.

3. *Resolutions:* returning to our daily responsibilities renewed, revitalized, and filled with resolutions that are practical and efficacious, thereby participating in the living spirit of Jesus Christ, entering into and effectively incarnating his sentiments and dispositions.

In one of his letters, De La Salle writes, "To my mind, what I must ask of God in prayer is that he tell me what he wants me to do and inspires me with the disposition he wants me to have."[32] While most of us are very aware of his trust in Providence, reading the events of his life as calls from God, for De La Salle, the "dispositions" of Jesus Christ are the other key element, because these are the agent of transformation, in line with the Bérullian

---

31 Since writing the introduction to the *Explanation*, Brother Donald Mouton has combined the *Recollection* dynamic that he described separately in his introduction with the awareness of the *Presence of God* dynamic. They are now seen together as a single dynamic that is the first of three. The three essential Lasallian prayer movements are also well described in the talk given by Brother Miguel Campos, FSC, to the 2006 International Mission Assembly, entitled "Fidelity to the Movement of the Holy Spirit" (Section 4.1). His contemporary application within the context of Lasallian discernment is wonderfully described and applied there. The talk may be found in Volume 3, No. 2 of the AXIS Journal of Lasallian Higher Education (*http://www.saintmarys.info/axis*).

32 De La Salle, John Baptist. *The Letters of John Baptist de La Salle.* Translation, introduction, and commentary by Colman Molloy, FSC. Edited with additional commentary by Augustine Loes, FSC. Landover, MD: Lasallian Publications, 1988, reprinted 2007: 248.

spirituality of the time.[33] This combination of trust in God's guidance through circumstances and events, and the cultivation of the sentiments and dispositions of Jesus, is still a captivating way of engaging one's faith today. De La Salle's interior prayer method provides steps for fostering such engagement, with the goal of entering into these sentiments and dispositions of Jesus Christ, being fully present in God's presence, becoming suffused with the Holy Spirit, and simply living attentively with God as present.

After describing a period of recollection—of settling ourselves into a broader, deeper, interior perspective of faith—De La Salle highlights three main means of becoming aware of God's presence: in the place where we are, in ourselves, and in a church. As the introduction explains, "These various ways do not create that presence, but rather enable us to recognize a presence that precedes us, a presence that is already there."[34] It calls to mind Jesus after the resurrection. "He is going ahead of you into Galilee. There you will see him." (Mk 16:7) God is always ahead, already there long before we arrive.

For each of the three means of becoming aware of God's presence that De La Salle highlights, two specific ways are provided, each explained with texts that weave in direct phrases from Scripture, along with examples of prayer exhortations that guide a person along the way. These six specific ways are like the answer that Golde, Tevye's wife in *Fiddler on the Roof* gives when he asks her, "Do you love me?" and Golde details the many things she has done for and with him over their 25 years of marriage, ending with the phrase, "If that's not love, what is?" In this case, De La Salle details how and where God's love, God's presence, is to be

---

33 The French School of Spirituality, initiated by Cardinal Pierre de Bérulle, stressed the necessity of one's personal *kenosis* (self-emptying) in order to be filled with Christ. The Christian made explicit acts of faith in the "principal Christian mysteries" (the Trinity, the Incarnation, the Redemption, and so on), incarnating the very being of Jesus by adopting actions and interior attitudes similar to those Christ first brought to reality by his every deed, every feeling, and every outlook—in terms used by the French School, his every "mystery" and "disposition." By entering into Christ's sentiments and dispositions, one entered into Christ's mystical reality of salvation and thereby came to act, and to be, more and more like him.

34 De La Salle, John Baptist. *Explanation of the Method of Interior Prayer.* Op. cit. Introduction, 8.

found, based on the Scriptures and his own long experience. He might likewise say, "If that's not God's presence, what is?"

- God is *present in the place where we are*. This can be considered in two ways.
  - God is everywhere (Ps 139:7–10, etc.).
  - Our Lord is present in the midst of those who are gathered in his name (Mt 18:20, etc.).

- God is *present within us*. This can be considered in two ways.
  - God maintains our existence (Acts 17, 28, etc.).
  - God is present through his grace and the Holy Spirit (Lk 17:21, etc.).

- God is *present in a church*. This can be considered in two ways.
  - A church is the house of God (Mt 21:12–13, etc.).
  - Our Lord is in the Most Blessed Sacrament [the Eucharist] (Rev 21:3, etc.).

For De La Salle, practicing awareness of God's presence is both the means and the goal of interior prayer, and simple attention is both the introduction and the final arrival into that presence.[35]

- "The first thing to be done in interior prayer is to become permeated with the presence of God through a sentiment of faith."[36]

---

35 Brother Joseph Schmidt, FSC, has commented that "Although St. La Salle may have been influenced by the Carmelite school of spirituality, and in particular by St. John of the Cross, in naming this way of prayer *simple attention*, there can be no doubt that his description of it was based on his own experience" (*Lasalliana* 05-A-31). The Carmelites were located in Reims, De La Salle's hometown, and we know that he made retreats with the Discalced Carmelites in 1686 (near Louviers), 1691, and 1706 (Rue Vaugirard, Paris). When De La Salle and two Brothers brought their educational ministry to Paris in 1688, he very likely became aware of, or already knew about, Brother Lawrence of the Resurrection (1614–1691), a Carmelite lay brother who lived at the Carmelite monastery near Rue Vaugirard for more than 50 years, and who was said to be held in high esteem by many learned people, religious, and priests because of his wisdom and insights into the practice of the presence of God. It would not be a stretch to believe that De La Salle met and spoke with Brother Lawrence at some point, or at least knew about publications of and about Brother Lawrence that appeared in 1692, 1694, 1699, and 1710, especially given their extensive popularity at the time.
36 De La Salle, John Baptist. *Explanation of the Method of Interior Prayer*. Op. cit., 59.

- "We can gradually acquire a certain facility for making ourselves aware of the presence of God by simple attention."[37]
- "Applying ourselves to the presence of God by simple attention consists in being before God with a simple, interior view of faith that God is present and remaining thus for some time."[38]
- "This simple attention procures inner consolation for the soul, which makes it find delight and joy in its awareness of the divine presence. The soul maintains this consolation without any need of other thoughts or reflections."[39]
- "[W]ays of engaging in interior prayer on a mystery, as also in considering the holy presence of God, can be related to the three stages of the spiritual life: discourses and multiple reasoning befit beginners; few and prolonged reflections befit the proficient; simple attention befits the advanced."[40]

This prayer of simple attention "seems to be the normal kind of prayer he expected his brothers to be drawn to."[41] It is a presence and disposition before God "with faith that God is present and remaining in a disposition of interior silence and affectionate attention."[42] This goal is achieved neither automatically nor quickly, two aspects that militate against its easy adoption in today's world, where speed and ease hold the upper motivational hand. Many years ago, one of my graduate school teachers was Sister Margaret Gorman, RSCJ, who taught the psychology of youth religious development. She made one of her most insightful comments at the end of a class where we were looking at a wide variety of developmental frameworks with their various "stages." She said: "Just because you know about the stages doesn't mean that you've gone through them." De La Salle would agree.

37 Ibid., 50.
38 Ibid., 51.
39 Ibid., 55.
40 Ibid., 97.
41 Ibid., Introduction, 11.
42 Ibid., Introduction, 4.

It would be fair to say that the steps or stages in De La Salle's interior prayer method are not completely rigorous. They are not like steps on a ladder, where one invariably follows the last. They are more like signposts on the road to the presence of God, similar to the yellow arrows found printed, carved, tiled, spray-painted, and scattered along the various *Camino* pilgrimage routes in Spain, all of them pointing to and leading to *Santiago de Compostela* and its shrine to Saint James. Interior prayer is more like a pilgrimage, something where both the journey and the goal are inextricably woven together. This deep connection between the universal presence of God and the pursuit of the presence of God is well made in the introduction to the *Explanation*: "The place De La Salle gives to the presence of God in his *Explanation* constitutes a distinctive characteristic of his method of interior prayer. In fact, the whole purpose of the method of interior prayer in De La Salle's view is to help us live every moment of life in the presence of God."[43] The frequent intentional recollection of the presence of God is one part of that training ground for developing a greater capacity for living in the presence of God.

Ultimately, practicing interior prayer and cultivating an ever-deeper awareness of the presence of God are two dimensions of the life of faith, which constituted the core of De La Salle's spiritual life. De La Salle wanted his followers to be completely filled with the spirit of faith. His meditations, exhortations, letters, and other writings, along with the witness of his life's journey, proclaim and support that single aim. In the *Rule* of the Brothers that De La Salle wrote in 1718, one section has been retained in all subsequent iterations of that *Rule,* because it describes this core element of the "story" of Lasallian education: "That which is of the utmost importance, and to which the greatest attention should be given in an Institute is that all who compose it possess the spirit peculiar to it. . . . The spirit of this Institute is first, a

---

43 Ibid., Introduction, 8.

spirit of faith, which should induce those who compose it not to look upon anything but with the eyes of faith, not to do anything but in view of God, and to attribute all to God."[44] There is, in effect, no difference between the spirit of faith and the spirit of interior prayer. They are identical faith stances before God, seen from two perspectives. "What simple attention is in the context of interior prayer, the spirit of faith is in the context of our daily lives. For De La Salle, the spirit of faith is simple attention 'in action.'"[45]

The Experience of the Holy Presence of God

For Saint John Baptist de La Salle, interior prayer is a habitual and intentional cultivation of exercising simple attention to God's presence. It "consists in being before God with a simple, interior view of faith that He is present."[46] Such an interior view of faith, cultivated through intentional reflective engagements with the virtues, teachings, and mysteries of Jesus, "leads the mind and heart to a sentiment of silent adoration, of love, of admiration, of gratitude and thanksgiving, of self-abasement and a desire of the heart to unite ourselves with our Lord."[47] It is very unlikely that De La Salle would have described interior prayer in this way without having experienced it himself, or that he would have recommended it to his Brothers unless he believed that it was a form of prayer that they would very likely be drawn to, even or especially when their daily labors were so demanding.[48]

It is all the more interesting, therefore, that a similarly directed element was folded into the prayer life of the school, most noticeably through the hourly invitations to recall the presence of God that punctuated the daily school schedule. In the words

---

44 Brothers of the Christian Schools. *The Rule of the Brothers of the Christian Schools*. Rome, Italy: Brothers of the Christian Schools, 2015: 11.
45 De La Salle, John Baptist. *Explanation of the Method of Interior Prayer*. Op. cit. Introduction, 12.
46 Ibid., 51.
47 Ibid., 97.
48 Ibid., Introduction, 11. This idea is developed further by Brother Joseph Schmidt, FSC, in *Lasalliana* 05-A-31.

of Brother Gerard Rummery, FSC, De La Salle "came to see that this recalling of God's presence was the cement that would bond teacher and student again and again in their common relationship with God. It was a reminder to the teachers of their duty as teachers; it was a reminder to pupils of their dignity as people made in the image and likeness of God."[49] Indeed, this shared presence of God with one's students is a hidden treasure of our Lasallian heritage. "It is not too strong to say that all Lasallian educators make God present to those confided to their care. At the same time, those present remind the educators that they are indeed in the presence of God."[50]

It is this living heritage of attending to God's presence in both prayer and ministry that has led Brothers, Lasallian educators, alums, and many others to appreciate and recognize God's presence in stories of their own. Those stories are well worth telling and well worth listening to, because they give testimony and life to the ongoing story of the Lasallian charism today.

Brother George Van Grieken, FSC[51]

49 Rummery, Gerard. *"Let Us Remember That We Are in the Holy Presence of God." AXIS: Journal of Lasallian Higher Education* (http://www.saintmarys.info/axis). Vol. 8, No. 3, 76.
50 Ibid., 77. Note especially the story that Brother Gerard Rummery, FSC, shares at the end of the article about the Muslim airline pilot, a former student of the Brothers in Alexandria, Egypt, and what he took away from the experience of regularly recalling the presence of God in school.
51 Brother George Van Grieken, FSC, is a De La Salle Christian Brother who is currently the director of the Lasallian Resource Center—*www.lasallianresources.org*. A graduate of Saint Mary's College of California (BA, MA) and of Boston College (PhD), he has worked as a classroom teacher and in Lasallian formation, vocation ministry, and school leadership, including most recently two years as president and CEO of St. Joseph's Institution International School in Singapore. His writings and workshops focus on Lasallian spirituality and formation, especially their application and integration within today's society and educational contexts.

Reflections

Instruments of God's Grace

It was sometime during the school year 2007–2008. It was a normal school day, and I was doing the usual thing—observing the class of a new teacher at La Salle Academy in Providence, Rhode Island. As I sat in the back of a United States history class, I noticed that the young man sitting next to me, a junior, did not have his textbook with him. During the 50-minute class he looked as if he were paying attention but seemed to do nothing but "look." At the end of class I saw him in the hallway and said to him (I did not know his name) that I expected more of him. And that was the start of a relationship that exists till this day.

During that year he frequently stopped by my office to chat or just to sit. At the end of the year he sent me a copy of an essay he was preparing for college admissions. In that essay he wrote about our budding relationship: "Talking with Brother Fred got me thinking. If his presence in my life meant so much to me, then maybe I can make a difference in other people's lives." Later in that essay he wrote about his relationship with God: "I believe that God put me here for a reason, and I want to be an instrument of his peace. Being close to God affects everything I do." I was moved by the actions of God in this young man's life and the way in which God used me as an instrument of grace.

However, it was early in his senior year that God's presence was revealed even more deeply. This now-senior stopped by my office after I had offered morning prayer for the school on the public address system. He remarked that he liked the prayer very much. I thanked him and asked him if he prayed. He said that of course he did. In fact, the night before he had written a prayer. I asked him if he would share the prayer with me. In typical teenage fashion he ripped a scrap of paper from his notebook, asked for a pencil, and wrote down his prayer. It read: "Let God's breeze pass through your window and fill your home so that not only you breathe him in, but everyone who enters." I was deeply moved by the words—so simple and yet so profound. He succinctly captured what it means when we say, "Let us remember that we are in the holy presence of God."

To this day that scrap of paper is under the glass on my desk, to be seen each morning as I bow down to kiss my desk and to remember that God is present—in this office, in each person who enters, in the depths of my own being. Over these years, this young man and his words have been instruments of God's grace in my life.

Brother Frederick C. Mueller, FSC
La Salle Academy, Providence, RI

A Line of Hugs

For about 20 years I was a member of a team of teachers instructing seventh- and eighth-grade students in all subject areas. We used books, films, field trips, and many hands-on experiences to integrate the various learning styles and multiple intelligences of our students. One year, in the middle of a unit about the Holocaust, a student, Selena, realized that a fourth-grade student on her school bus wore a yarmulke. She asked Daniel if he was Jewish. When he responded affirmatively, she questioned him on his knowledge of the Holocaust. Daniel told her that he had heard something about it, but really did not know much. He then told her that his grandmother, who lived with him, often spoke to groups about the Holocaust. Selena immediately asked him to see if his grandmother would come and speak to our three classes. Daniel's grandma was delighted and called the principal to arrange for a special assembly.

On the day of the visit, Daniel got permission to attend the assembly, since he had never heard his grandmother speak in public. The small group of 36 students and eight adults met in our gathering space to hear her tale. Grandma explained that she was one of the "hidden children" featured in a documentary produced by Steven Spielberg, in collaboration with others, to tell the story of Jewish children who were smuggled out of Nazi Germany and hidden in foreign countries until the end of World War II. Grandma recalled walking with her mom and older brother to a train station to see her father off, since he was being sent to a "work camp." She said that as she was waving goodbye to him, she did not realize that it would be the last time that she would ever see him. (Daniel was seated in the first row of the assembly and held a box of tissues. His grandmother assured him she would need tissues as she recounted her story.)

We watched as Grandma picked up a cloth bag and removed a tiny embroidered dress. It was the dress she wore as a five-year-old, when her mother took her to the very same train station a week later to join hundreds of children who were taken by a humanitarian group on a "trip" to an unknown destination. She recalled that she spent the next few years with a family in what she later found out was Belgium. She and two other children stayed in an attic on most days, but they were regularly allowed to play outside for a few hours. The war ended, and these "orphans" had a difficult time being reunited with their families. Some never found any surviving relatives.

As Daniel's grandmother told her tale of eventually finding her mother and brother, who had survived a concentration camp, she wiped her eyes often. The reunited family emigrated to the United States and later to Israel, but Grandma married, raised a family, and settled in New York. She told the children that she now spends time telling others about the Holocaust so that it will never happen again.

It was extremely quiet in the room when she opened the floor to questions. A single hand hesitantly went up. It was Daniel's friend, Selena. She asked in a very wobbly voice, "Would it be alright if I gave you a hug?" When Grandma nodded through her tears, one by one the students got in line and each silently hugged this woman who had gone through so much. We were most assuredly in the holy presence of God.

Elizabeth "Betty" Williams
Martin de Porres Schools, New York

A Community of Prayer

In De La Salle's Meditation for the Feast of St. Theresa, he wrote, "If you love God, prayer will be the food of your soul, and God will enter within you and will have you eat at his table. . . . You will then have the advantage of having God present in your actions and of having no other purpose than to please him." (Med. 177.3)

When I was hired at Calvert Hall more than 20 years ago, we had a chaplain on staff. In addition to monthly school Mass, he would celebrate daily Mass a couple of times a week. However, about 10–15 years ago, due to the declining number of available clergy in our diocese, our school chaplain was reassigned. While we still have priests in our area come to celebrate schoolwide liturgies, we missed the regular celebration of the Mass during the week. Several members of our religion department decided that we should instead offer a daily prayer opportunity before school. We started offering daily Communion services each morning before homeroom. This has now been our tradition for quite a number of years. For the last two academic years, we have added the recitation of the Teacher's Prayer at the conclusion of the service.

While this new endeavor filled my spiritual and physical hunger for the Eucharist, my call as a Lasallian to ground myself in the holy presence of God is filled in the "community" that gathers for prayer. On any given morning, six to eight faculty members, along with a handful of students, gather to pray, reflect on the daily readings, and receive Holy Communion. This "community" has become a "family" as we regularly laugh together, at times cry together, and most certainly uplift one another in prayer together.

Four of us rotate the responsibility of leading the service and offering a reflection on the daily readings. Each of us, in our own style, tries to apply the readings to both the life of the teacher, and more importantly, to the life of the students. We try to find a spiritual kernel of truth that the community gathered for prayer can take with them as they go about their day, walking in "the holy presence of God."

"Your work does not consist in making your disciples to be Christians but in helping them to be true Christians. . . . To give this spirit to others, you have to possess it well." (Med. 171.3) We are a small church, a community or family of faith. We share each other's burdens, challenges, and joys. We challenge one another's behaviors when they seem contrary to the Gospel. It can become easy to fill my time each morning with the busyness of teaching (emails, lesson plans, faculty room gossip, and so on), but I am a better, more effective Lasallian when I nourish myself with the holy presence of God found both in Holy Communion and in my Holy Community.

"To you especially Jesus Christ addresses these words of today's Gospel: Seek first the Kingdom of God. You ought not to have come to this community except to seek here the reign of God: first, for you, and second, for those whose instruction God has entrusted to you." (Med. 67.1)

To bring God's holy presence to my students, I first need to bring God's presence TO and INTO me.

Chris Barczak
Calvert Hall College High School,
Baltimore, MD

You Could Help

"I am sure looking forward to things getting back to normal around here," my husband said at breakfast that morning.

Things were winding down after a crazy-busy summer. I had recently taken over a new role at the Saint Mary's University of Minnesota, and summer was the busiest time of year for my office. I was new to the position, running short-staffed, and averaging close to 60 work hours a week. Our adult son had moved home temporarily and was in the process of moving out. And we had just buried a very dear, elderly friend, for whom we had been caring. I was ready for a break. "Normal" sounded wonderful!

Fast forward to the afternoon. One of my student workers walked into my office with a young lady in tow. He said he was hoping that I could help her. She was transferring to SMU and had no place to stay until school started in a few weeks. Issues at home had forced her out, and she found herself homeless. Would we take her in?

I immediately started thinking of all the reasons I could not possibly do this. I was tired. My son had just moved out, and the extra room was a mess. I was still grieving the loss of my dear friend. Things were winding down at work, but I was still very busy. Plus, it's not easy taking in someone you don't know!

I apologized, promising that I would try and think of someone who could help, and sent them on their way. As soon as my office door closed behind them, I heard an inner voice say, "You could help!" "I'm tired!!" I answered back. Then I clearly heard that same voice say, "To whom much is given, much is expected." Darn! I was being called out in a big way!

Reluctantly, I got up from desk, stepped out of my office, and told them that she could stay with us. Even though I was not 100 percent on board with what I was doing, once I saw her look of relief and gratitude, I knew I had made the right decision.

We may have opened our home to her, but she opened our hearts in so many ways. The more we got to know her and hear her story, the more we knew that God had put her in our path for a reason.

I am now glad that I listened to God and had the courage to trust God enough to get past my reluctance, to "step out of the boat" in faith. Our lives are now blessed with the inclusion of this amazing young woman, someone who, I know, will accomplish wonderful things.

Her goal is to get a degree from Saint Mary's University, one that will allow her to "help other people." Think of the ripple effect. . . . God is good!

Katherine Pederson
Saint Mary's University of Minnesota,
Winona, MN

Safe, Appreciated, Loved

Young men come to our residential youth and family service agencies for many reasons: abuse, neglect, addiction, domestic violence, sexual victimization, criminal activity, and the like. Each needs to be loved for who they are and for the goodness and potential that may be seen behind the rags they wear and the troubles they carry as part of their tattered life stories.

It was Holy Week, and some 40 Brothers had gathered for a retreat at this center that is also home to a child welfare agency. Earlier that week, a young man had arrived into the program. It was a challenging transition for an only child suddenly away from home and living with 30 others. Fear, anxiety, and the telltale signs of a troubled and perhaps abusive background: staring at the floor, no eye contact, speaking in a whisper, quiet—almost silent—but not due to shyness, withdrawn, jumpy if someone gets too close, "Please do not touch me." But Lasallian care is special, relational, and healing.

This young man was in our culinary arts program and assigned to the Brothers' Dining Room for the retreat. The Brothers, guests, and regulars greeted him, asked him his name and a bit about him, talked to him in casual conversation, and just showed personal care at each meal during those holy days.

We watched eye contact beginning to be made, withdrawn silence replaced with a quiet "Hello, Brother" at the fourth or fifth meal, then a joke shared and a smile as a Brother said, "Thank you; good job." At the last meal of the retreat, this young man shook hands with his Brothers, a smile on his face, and a bit of confidence in himself. This was perhaps the most important and valuable type of ministering that we do: healing parts of the past with simple caring, respect, and perhaps even a bit of love.

The Brothers cared and touched a heart in need just by being themselves, and a young man felt, perhaps for the first time in a very long time, safe, appreciated, cared for and, dare I say, loved. God is made present and lives are transformed through caring relationships—perhaps more than we know.

Brother James Martino, FSC
Ocean Tides School, Narragansett, RI

The Fire of a Double Passion

Our Lasallian spirituality makes us open to reality and to its needs with the eyes of God, with the gaze of God. Pope Francis tells us that our relationship with God is a play of glances. The spirit of faith and zeal plays a unifying role for us that makes us see reality, not as profane or sacred, but as a sacramental. Everything reveals God to us. We "recognize Jesus beneath the poor rags of the children" (Med. 96.3). The school, "the work of God," becomes a theological place where the Brother, through his concrete and effective love for the young, makes the face of God visible, which is why today we are talking about a mysticism with open eyes.

For our spirituality, this means that the world, far from being an obstacle to our encounter with God, is the normal way in which God manifests himself to us: as presence or absence, but always from the initiative of his gratuitous love. "God so loved the world that he gave his only Son" (Jn 3:16). And the world is, at the same time, the place where we must prolong that presence.

Our participation in the glory and life of the Trinity makes us followers of Jesus, sent from the Father, and witnesses of the love of the Father revealed in Jesus, with the power of the Spirit for the life of the world. This experience, both contemplative and charged with action, makes us feel, in the words of Teilhard de Chardin, like children of heaven and children of the earth in deep inner unity, without the one drowning out the other. That is why we must carry in our hearts the fire of a double passion: a passion for God and a passion for the children and young people who God puts in our hands, especially the most vulnerable, the least loved, those who do not find a meaning for their fragile lives.

I experienced this in a very special way during the years that I lived in Guatemala, where there was a real persecution against the Church, and where the Brothers suffered the consequences of our work with poor indigenous youth. It was during these years that Brother James Miller gave testimony with his blood of his deep love for young people. As director of the Santiago Indigenous Institute of Guatemala City, a place that prepared rural teachers for the whole country, I was able to discover God through the poor, simple people, full of human values, and especially from their sufferings. Those crucified people revealed to me a God who gave his life for us until the end, and who, despite everything, is always close to the least and the most vulnerable.

I make mine the words of Elie Wiesel when he tells us, in his book *Night*,[1] of his first night in the Auschwitz concentration camp. Faced with the terrible prospect of a child's execution, he shares with us his feelings as a 14-year-old Jewish boy as he hears a man ask, "For God's sake, where is God?" Wiesel recalls: "And from within me, I heard a voice answer: 'Where He is? This is where—hanging here from this gallows. . . .'" Yes, God was in our more than 30 indigenous teachers who were killed in those years. God was in the testimony of love and dedication of Brother James Miller, and of so many religious men and women who offered their lives. God was in the thousands of orphans, innocent victims of the conflict, and abused women. God was in all those who worked for peace.

This was an experience of God's presence in my life that I will never forget.

∾

Brother Álvaro Rodríguez Echeverría, FSC
District of Central America

---

1 Wiesel, Elie. *Night.* Edited and with an introduction by Harold Bloom. Bloom's Guides. New York, NY: Infobase Publishing, 2009: 116.

WEEK

7

God Is Always Among Us

Dr. Ware, my theology professor, often spoke of the power of language. How else could God have created the heavens and the earth simply through "God said"? Why else did Jacob desire Isaac's blessing? Why else does John tell us, "In the beginning was the Word . . ."? Now, when I think of the power of language, I ask, how else do three words, "Let us remember," quiet a gym of 500 rambunctious students gathered for an assembly. The response is immediate—silence—as 500 almost feral students are transformed into 500 almost angelic students, responding, "We are always in the holy presence of God." Oops, you might say . . . always? Yes, always.

After 9/11, the Class of 2002 memorialized our nation's tragedy with a large rock, now the focal point of a serene prayer garden that welcomes all who arrive at our school. On one side is engraved, "In memory of the victims of September 11, 2001." On the other side, "Let us remember that we are always in the holy presence of God." And there we have it. "Always." In stone.

Why we began including the word "always" is a mystery to me, a mystery with which I am quite comfortable. "Always" became part of my soul when, as the speaker for the "Obstacles to God's Friendship" talk at Kairos, I challenged the participants to respect themselves and each other, to respect our retreat space, and to respect the spirit of Kairos itself. I reminded them of what we as Lasallians say at the beginning of each day. "Let us remember that we are always in the holy presence of God." And though we end our prayer with "Live Jesus in our hearts . . . Forever!" we are still in God's loving presence, whether we are in prayer or not. Wherever we are is a holy place, for God is always among us, and therefore we are able to participate in God's extraordinary work.

Part of this extraordinary work is to help others remember God's abiding presence. This is relevant for us because we have had two teachers and one student diagnosed with cancer in the last two years. During that time, a student and I asked members of the Prayer Shawl Ministry at our church for shawls for these three. Having been a recipient of a prayer shawl, I know the power of these shawls, which are created with loving hands, blessed, and then given to those who are going through difficult times.

To combine these two aspects of "Let us remember"—the spoken reminder that we are always in the holy presence of God, and the physical reminder of the shawl itself—we created a Prayer Shawl Ministry at St. Michael's. As we begin the first stitch of each shawl and scarf for the homeless, we recite those powerful words, "Let us remember," and remind the recipients that they, too, are always in the holy presence—and in the loving arms—of God.

Janis Chitwood
Saint Michael's High School,
Santa Fe, NM

It Started with Flashcards

I can still picture it as clearly as if it happened yesterday. We were in our second year at the San Miguel Middle School in Minneapolis, and a sixth-grader named Marco had enrolled. We quickly discovered that not only did Marco know very little English, but he was also illiterate in Spanish.

So, there I was, president of San Miguel and working with him for about 45 minutes three times a week. I was showing him simple one-syllable words on flashcards: *Them, Look, Talk*. Marco struggled, but we made progress. Fast-forward to his eighth-grade graduation.

I was sitting on stage, and Marco got up to do one of the readings at the graduation service. He made it through, and he read well. I remember tearing up, and at that moment, it all came together for me: San Miguel existed so that a student such as Marco could have an opportunity for salvation. Here he was, a poised young man who could barely read only a couple years before, now prepared to take on the next challenge, saved from an existence that would have denied him access to so much that life has to offer. This is exactly what the Founder intended, and at that graced moment God's holy presence shining through Marco warmed my heart and buoyed my spirit.

Brother Larry Schatz, FSC
Christian Brothers of the Midwest

The Collective Lived Spirit of God's Presence

The person who inspired me to join the Lasallian mission was Brother Michael Collins. He could command a presence when he walked into any room, and he had the kind of charisma that people naturally gravitated toward.

One afternoon in the spring, as I was in the middle of an English lesson with my eighth-graders at the Catholic grade school where I taught in the archdiocese, Brother Michael suddenly flung the door open. The students knew who he was by reputation, and he declared that he was here to see if this "Brothers' Boy" could teach. After the class, when the students had left, he walked up to me at the podium and said, "It is time for you to come home—your heart is at DeLaSalle."

Five years later, after I had accepted Brother's invitation and started as a teacher at DeLaSalle, Brother Michael passed away unexpectedly midyear. Like many in our school community, we were in shock that this larger-than-life man could have gone so quickly. The evening after Brother had passed away, I remember holding my newborn son in my arms and having this feeling of being scared. A feeling of uncertainty and the unknown was starting to take hold over my spirit.

Not too long after, my phone rang, and I did not recognize the number. Atypical of me, I opted to answer the phone and see who it was. When I said my "Hello," the response was one of intercession from our patron, Saint John Baptist de La Salle. The person said, "Hello, this is Brother Milton from Totino-Grace. I do not know you well, but I know that you and your community are hurting. If you need anything, please lean on us for support."

That night, we spoke on the phone for more th.
and my sense of uneasiness began to evolve into a spii.
and togetherness. That conversation began a friendship thai
still endures today. But more importantly, I experienced the
collective lived spirit of God's presence through "together and
by association."

Like our Founder, Saint John Baptist de La Salle, we constantly strive to identify and implement gospel values in our work
and in our relationships. The lived examples of Brother Michael,
Brother Milton, and countless other Lasallians inspire me and
others to fulfill our global mission.

Patrick A. Felicetta
DeLaSalle High School, Minneapolis, MN

Love Is the Foundation

My last week in my final year at the Buttimer Institute of Lasallian Studies was cut short due to sudden multifocal strokes, which had previously left me disabled and unable to continue my treasured ministry of teaching—a passion for over 45 years. When returning from Buttimer, the phrase, "Let us remember the holy presence of God," always became more embedded in my heart and in the heart of my prayer with students and staff. That act of "remembering God's presence" has now traveled out of the high school setting into a more personal classroom, where, again, God is trying to teach me that relying on His presence will bring about my salvation and, through witness, the salvation of others I encounter.

There is a new ministry slowly unfolding for me; new lessons of relying on God's Spirit to lead and comfort are a daily assignment, although not without occasional failures on my part to put them into action. For Saint John Baptist de La Salle, a similar instruction must have taken place, particularly in his later years. Throughout his entire journey, his "remembering" enabled him to create this Lasallian ministry of learning and this community of educators.

The call to apostolic spirituality looks different for me now in 2017. But the personal meaning remains the same, as I reflected back in 2015 while attending the Buttimer Institute.

Please God, may I continue to heed and follow:

The Call

An unfamiliar knock raps softly on my heart-door;
It's late, and I have already tucked away my plans for
    the coming days.
Barely audible, the knock persists, and I stumble
    begrudgingly to answer.
Ruah, the Spirit, calls, and I seek to obey.
The love of Christ compels me . . . propels me forward.

The Need

"They need a teacher, an instructor?" I ask.

"No, they need salvation; whole understanding—they
need an educator—someone to lead them out of
ignorance—a sense of meaninglessness—and into a
lived understanding of how much they are loved by
Me; how I desire wholeness and fullness of life for them
and for you."

Signum Fidei: Sign of Faith

As Mary did, I press for details: "How can this be since
I do not know them?"

"The Spirit will come and overshadow you. Trust and
establish relationships. First, you must know Me—be in
relationship with Me—then teach by example. Have the
humility and vulnerability to really see them and allow
them to see you."

Human Education

"Seek to give freely, give them a human education: feed their spirits, teach them to pray, awaken their senses, form a community, show them you care. Give them a chance to become a Human Dynamic: move through the cognitive, empower by the affective, and live in the behavioral."

"Above all, remember that LOVE is the foundation: Together and by Association!"

Leda E. Reeves
West Catholic Preparatory High School,
Philadelphia, PA

Thankful for the Encounter

Charles was quiet, polite, and amiable. However, he was either unable or unwilling to do the assignments. He did little outside of class, but that isn't unique when freshmen experience the freedom of college. His test scores were regularly at the bottom of the distribution. From his behavior it seemed as if this course was not a priority. The withdrawal deadline was approaching, so I asked to see him in my office. I suggested that since the likelihood of success in this class was minimal, withdrawal was an option to seriously consider.

I didn't expect the response that I received. "Please don't make me withdraw from this class!"

I explained that I couldn't make him withdraw, but what good would an F in the course do?

"I know that I've failed you, my family, and myself, but please don't make me withdraw! I don't want to be like my father."

He fought the tears welling up in his eyes. I wondered if he felt that his father gave up on things too easily. Then I learned that his father wasn't around much as he grew up. Drugs were more important to him than family.

More spilled out. He was the first in his family to attend college. Then came what I considered the most devastating admission. The grandmother who had raised him repeatedly told him that he couldn't succeed in college. He seemed to have no one who believed in him, although he mentioned an uncle who provided occasional refuge.

"How are your other classes going?" I asked. "Could we consider a major that isn't as dependent on math? Can you stay with your uncle more?"

I prayed that I might find some words of encouragement and support. I felt the presence of God in his struggles. Charles was one of God's innocents. That he trusted me with his story was a wonderful God-given privilege.

I still hope that listening and being present helped. My understanding of his dilemma did not mean that a miracle occurred and he passed the class. But he did not withdraw, and he attended through the final exam. I remember him, and I pray for him, and I wonder about the outcome. Did that college degree that meant so much help him to feel more secure? Did he find his passion so that a job would be more than work? Is he now the father that he wished his father had been for him?

Ultimately, I must be thankful for the encounter, entrusting him and all of our students to the care of God.

***

Cathy Grilli
Christian Brothers University, Memphis, TN

Giving Their Pain to God

"What if I am mad at God? Can I share that?" Valeria asked.

"Of course," I responded.

And so started a shared prayer activity on a Kairos retreat that I will never forget. Seven students sitting on the floor in a darkened room with only a lit candle—representing the light of Christ—and our small group cross, representing God's sacrifice for us. Each student was about to address God directly with a prayer.

"Well then let me start," Marcela interrupted. She grabbed the cross and shared how angry she was with God for not providing her a father at home. Hers was a gang member who had been in and out of prison and a drug user. Tears welled up in her eyes.

Alexa went next. "I wish God had not taken my mom away from me." Her mom had died from cancer a few years earlier, and her dad was not at home. Instead, he was living in the Tenderloin in San Francisco, battling drugs and depression. More tears.

Finally the cross came back to Valeria. "I miss my mother too. Why would a loving God allow her to be killed?" Her mom had been violently murdered by her father as she and her sister watched in horror.

Now the whole group was weeping, myself included. Clearly, the walls were broken. The anger released. The healing process could now begin.

I felt the presence of the Holy Spirit engulf all in a loving embrace. From that moment forward all three girls had an entirely new perspective on their life journeys. They began to understand that God is present even in the most difficult or heart-wrenching situations; even when God's answer is not what they wanted to hear.

Giving their pain to God freed them to live their lives more fully. And God was present again in their lives. They began to truly feel God's love in their lives. Plus sharing with their small group bonded them with others who could support them.

I think about that moment often, knowing that although each will never be totally whole again, those three students had a huge burden taken off their shoulders. Their paradigms shifted; maybe just slightly, but they did shift. De La Salle tells us, "You carry out a work that requires you to touch hearts." Hearts were touched in that memorable moment, especially mine.

Greg Schmitz
Sacred Heart Cathedral Preparatory,
San Francisco, CA

Indefinable, Mysterious, Inseparable

When we believe, even in doubt, we never lose hope. In our occasional moments of discouragement, sometimes provoked by failures or misunderstandings, or which occur slowly and apparently without reason, and which often disappear in the same way, we do not feel ourselves drifting into the void. Something, someone brings us back to life, never letting us detach ourselves from the central core of our existence. We feel a presence, even if it is indefinable, mysterious, yet inseparable from who we are; a presence that is part of ourselves. This is what I call the presence of God, and it is something that I have often experienced.

I was exactly 13 years old when I heard the sentence, "Let us remember . . .," for the first time. It was in a class at the very beginning of the school year. The sentence was repeated to us regularly, on the hour, if I remember correctly. We were immersed in a very religious atmosphere. I don't know if this would have been the case five or ten years later. Maybe, but I am not sure, because people became more cautious at the evocation of anything religious, at least in our little world. But never was the invitation completely forgotten, even though it was rarely invoked during the school years that followed. The presence of God remained as a given! This mantra was truly my first contact with the Lasallian world.

When we hear or watch the news today, it is not the presence of God that we are reminded of, but all too often, alas, that of evil, of human stupidity, of fanaticism, of ignorance, of injustice, of unconsciousness in the face of our common environmental responsibility. What we see very often is the seeming victory of pettiness, exploitation of the vulnerable, a race for short-term profit without worrying about the long-term consequences. Despite all the good reasons we may have for despairing of the human species, we must stay the course with hope: Let us remember that we are in the holy presence of God! It is this presence that changes everything and that has often prevented me, especially when I was younger, from falling away morally. It was a veritable lifesaver, because it was a loving presence.

In the words of André Frossard: "Were we to spend a thousand centuries in the presence of God, we would only experience it as though for the first time."

Brother Florent Gaudreault, FSC
District of Francophone Canada

The Commonness
of Everyday Things

Past the wineries and the many acres of orchards, grapes, hops, and mint in the Yakima Valley, you will find a world of two extremes—extreme wealth and privilege, and extreme poverty and hardship—that coexist in some cases literally only blocks from one another. Because ours is a region rich in agriculture, it is also one with a large population of immigrants—those who venture into Central Washington in order to plant, tend to, and harvest our valley's bounty. While they may be living side by side, these worlds are separated by a cultural divide that is as wide as the distance these immigrants take to travel from Mexico and South America to work in the rich agricultural fields and orchards of the Yakima Valley.

Every day, for the past 20 years, La Salle High School has worked to bring the children of those extremes together to study, to walk together on their faith journey, to join in their commitment to serve others, and, most importantly, to help build their futures. Every hour of every school day, children of non-English speaking immigrant parents walk hand in hand, arm in arm, laughing, talking, and studying with those of Yakima's more privileged class. These young people are learning from each other and developing friendships that will last a lifetime. They are now returning to their communities to make a difference.

Laura is one of those graduates. Laura arrived in the Yakima Valley as a baby, the daughter of immigrant parents searching for a better life. After St. Joseph's grade school in Sunnyside, where the mean household income is 39 percent lower than the national average, Laura came to La Salle through the sponsorship of a caring benefactor in our community. At La Salle, Laura's leadership qualities blossomed!

Karl Rahner speaks of God's presence as times when "the very commonness of everyday things harbors the eternal marvel and silent mystery of God." At La Salle in Yakima, the very commonness of everyday things has now helped hundreds of students like Laura have a future that they couldn't have imagined! Each day we see the "eternal marvel and silent mystery of God" as we find ways to open the door of a quality education to the "poor and working class." Joined together with those more financially well-off students, we open hearts and minds of all toward a more fulfilling life.

As for Laura, she went on to attend Loyola Marymount University where she majored in political science and sociology. Her journey included leadership initiatives at Harvard and advocacy work for the Latino Caucus in the California State Senate. She now works as deputy press secretary for a California state senator and will be assisting his national senate campaign efforts. Not too bad for an immigrant girl from Sunnyside, Washington!

Tim McGree
La Salle High School of Yakima,
Union Gap, WA

The Helpers in Our Midst

Gods holy presence has never been stronger in my professional educational experience than when a tragedy has occurred
in the school community. In my 12 years as a Lasallian educator,
tragedy has struck my high school several times. We have had
students die through car accidents, health issues, and suicide. We
have had parents die much too early. We most recently encountered wildfires that closed the school for two weeks, wildfires that
took the homes and property of many students and faculty. It's
strange to say, but I have never experienced a stronger community feeling than when these tragedies have struck. Why is that?

It's not that people don't care for each other and help in the
everyday. They do, and the extraordinary is present in the ordinary. However, tragedy can bring out the best in others and
demonstrate God's presence in very life-giving and visible ways.
The opportunity to care for our fellow human beings is simply too
great to resist in these moments.

Mr. Fred Rogers told this story: "When I was a boy and I
would see scary things in the news, my mother would say to
me, 'Look for the helpers. You will always find people who are
helping.' To this day, especially in times of 'disaster,' I remember
my mother's words and I am always comforted by realizing that
there are still so many helpers—so many caring people in this
world." The helpers in each of the cases that I'm reminded of were
ever-present. In those times of tragedy, there were many teachers who stepped up to speak, lead prayer, provide meals, offer
hugs, give assignment extensions, and ask the simple question,
"What can I do to help you right now?" There were students who

planned donation drives, wrote cards of comfort, made posters with messages of love, and asked the simple question, "What can I do to help right now?"

When there is stress, grief or darkness, the natural, beautiful, and instinctual desire to help from these students and others, based on a love of the neighbor, is the greatest beacon of hope and light. The helper in our midst is Christ in our midst. The helper in our midst is the physical presence of God's love, and the priority of the relationships found in our Lasallian community.

Who are the helpers in your midst? Take a moment to praise God and your community members for their holy presence in your midst.

Andy Hodges
Justin-Siena High School, Napa, CA

Solidarity and Compassion

It was a typical weekday, about two weeks into being a seventh grader at De La Salle Academy. Many things were still new to me: getting used to the friendly environment of the community, rigorous academic expectations, and living in the United States for only three years.

I still remember this day so vividly. Sitting in my language arts class, I saw Brother Brian, the founder and principal of the school, walk in quietly and calmly select a few students: "You, you, and you—come with me. Pack your bag." The students started looking around, not knowing what was going on. My teacher continued teaching, which then made the students focus back on the class.

This happened throughout the next period as well. We students started making assumptions that the chosen students were those who hadn't finished their summer homework and got sent home. "But that can't be! She ALWAYS does her home-work," one student said about a student that was sent home. There was another strand of rumor—this one with humor—that the teachers were aliens and were abducting us! We all giggled and were half-hoping to be called, so that we would know what was going on.

Finally it was my turn. Brother Brian called me, and I thought, "This isn't about the summer homework—I handed mine in!" When we reached his office, Brother Brian introduced me to a lady whose son was in the sixth grade. He told us that David Martinez's mom was going to take some of us home since something had happened in lower Manhattan, and all subways were closed for now. On our way out of the school, I saw many people making their way uptown. The scene looked like a marathon, but in slow motion—a gravely silent atmosphere. It was a bizarre scene. On our way home in the car, we sang a few Disney songs as David's mom dropped each and every one of us at our homes. When I arrived at my Bronx apartment, there was a scene of smoking buildings falling like Lego blocks being shown on the television. It was September 11, 2001. I sat in front of the screen, watching the surreal replay of the buildings falling down.

Ten years later I graduated from college and joined the De La Salle family as a volunteer, and later returned to my own school as a teacher. The school had been holding an annual memorial service since 2001, and I was able to join in that service exactly 10 years from the day described above. During the service, Brother Brian spoke about the effects of terrorism, and that the way to defy hatred was by standing up for what is right. He spoke about the way that the school had decided to handle the situation on that September 11. Instead of dumping the fear and frustration of the adults on the students, each teacher was informed of the situation and was asked to carry on during the day as best as possible. We were not bombarded with anxiety, stress, or anger. That is exactly what the terrorists would have wanted: to influence the victims not only physically but also psychologically and spiritually. Brother Brian was determined to lessen that stress and possible breakdown, which I realized was another way of fighting against terrorism.

That same year, another faculty member joined the family. He introduced himself as Wilson Martinez, and he would be teaching Spanish. He also mentioned that he was the father of alumnus David Martinez. My heart instantly jumped. I walked towards him, introduced myself, and told him about the day when his wife took me home safely. We just held our hands in silence, with overwhelming feelings of solidarity and compassion.

The holy presence of God truly lived in our hearts, not just on that specific day. It has worked in each and every one of us on a daily basis. We continue to do our best to share the love that we received as family members of De La Salle.

Soobin Lim
De La Salle Academy, New York, NY

You People Aren't Like
Most People I Know

De La Salle Vocational serves young men who have been adjudicated as delinquent by the family court of Philadelphia. The students attending the program are committed nonvoluntarily and receive a traditional high school academic curriculum, career and technical education programming, and social work services. The students are often not happy to be assigned to the program and typically enter very resistant to the care that we are seeking to provide.

Charles was one such young man. He was angry to have been arrested, frustrated to have been removed from his neighborhood school, and infuriated that a probation officer would be monitoring his behavior. He was also fully enamored with street life and the violence associated with it. His one strength upon admission was that he attended the program daily.

I often had the unenviable task of attempting to redirect his negative behaviors and calm his boundless enthusiasm for creating negative situations. I also chaired staff meetings where there would often be a push for harder consequences for Charles, in order to ensure his compliance with program expectations. In these same staff meetings, teachers would also acknowledge his intelligence and strong academic and vocational abilities. The lament at the end of these meetings usually was, "If he could only channel all of that energy on his school work, he could accomplish great things."

In the spring of 2011, after almost two years in the program, Charles had earned enough credits to be within a couple months of graduation. During this time, he was participating in an outdoor science experiment and decided that it would be a good idea to throw tiny stones at his instructor. One of the stones hit the instructor in the back of the head.

Following this incident the administration received pressure from our faculty and staff to remove Charles from our program and refer him back to the court for placement with another agency. The dean and I met with him and his grandmother. During that meeting, Charles very quietly yet sincerely asked us to allow him to stay, because he wanted to graduate and knew that this would not be guaranteed if he went to another agency. He said that he would publicly apologize to the teacher and would not create any further problems. We then took the matter to a team meeting, one that involved all the staff who were working with him. Everyone agreed to let him continue at De La Salle. While he was far from perfect after that meeting, he did settle down significantly and spent his last two months highly focused on earning the final credits that he needed for graduation.

In early June, the day before graduation, I was standing in the hallway with Charles' social worker when Charles walked up to us with a strange look on his face. We asked him why he had that look, and he said, "You know you people aren't like most people I know." We asked him what he meant by that, and he said, "You don't get mad, you usually have positive attitudes, and you give guys a lot of chances. This isn't like any other place where I've been. Thanks."

All of the work he accomplished in the two years he was with us culminated in his graduation the following day.

James Logan
Saint Francis – Saint Vincent Homes,
Philadelphia, PA

Be Faithful—I'm Not in Charge

My first memory of Thomas was his weak handshake—a complete dead fish attached to a wrist and forearm. He was referred to my office by a concerned teacher.

He sat down, his eyes dropping to the floor and his shoulders slumping, as if even the effort of needing to stay upright was more than he could muster.

"Thomas, can you tell me about what happened in class today?"

Silence.

"Thomas, how are you feeling right now?"

His left leg began to shake.

"Thomas, you are in a safe place. Nothing bad can happen to you here."

He looked up, just briefly, unsure of whether to believe me or not.

Thomas was back in my office the next day and the day after that. On the days that he didn't stay home from school, he was likely to be with me at some point.

Many times, Thomas came to my office so overwhelmed with anxiety and depression that he would curl up into the fetal position, hugging his knees so tightly that I knew he was trying to disappear.

Outside therapists became involved. Psychiatrists prescribed medications, often making Thomas so nauseated that he would hunch over in agony, his already emaciated frame overcome by these powerful drugs.

Some days the haze would lift, and I'd gain some insight into Thomas—struggles with family, outside pressures, personal identity. But soon, the window would close and the fog would return. On many days, my greatest accomplishment was getting Thomas to stand and walk to class with me, his legs wobbly under the weight of his backpack and the weight of his pain.

I thought often of Saint John Baptist de La Salle's exhortation that touching the hearts of students is the greatest miracle we can perform. And yet I had no evidence that anything I tried with Thomas was making a shred of difference.

Eventually, we met with Thomas's family to inform them that we could no longer meet his needs. Thomas's mother wept softly throughout the meeting, the unimaginable depth of her pain showing plainly on her face. I was able to make it back to my office before I did the same.

All of the hours that I spent with Thomas felt like a failure. I wasn't able to help him, and helping is my job description, my vocation. What had I missed? What else could I have done? Did I make any difference at all?

It was my colleague Cris who reminded me that experiencing the holy presence of God is not simply about the good times, the success stories. It's always about the journey. It's about the meeting and walking with others in their pain, in their doubt, and in their suffering, and knowing that that's our call.

Thomas touched my heart in a profound way. I now hope that I was able to do the same for him in some small way.

The holy presence of God humbles me constantly, reminds me that I'm not in charge, that my work is simply to be faithful.

And when I forget that, I am lucky to be blessed by the wisdom of other Lasallians who are trying their best to do the same. I am lucky that they are there to remind me to *Remember*.

Scott Drain
De La Salle High School, Concord, CA

19

A Source of Light
and Strength

D e La Salle's spirituality in some ways resembles that of St.
Thérèse of Lisieux's childhood. De La Salle invites us to live
in all simplicity one of the daily essential elements of our lives: the
continual presence of God.

Throughout my career, I have had the privilege of teaching
young people at many different grade levels, including 30 years
at the university level. I owe them so much, having adopted the
insight of our Founder to consider this beautiful profession as
"a ministry" (*Rule* 2, 16). Moreover, I like a reflection from our
Superior General, Brother Robert Schieler, FSC: "Why are we
being asked to be more attentive to the poor, the excluded, and
the marginalized on the peripheries, the deserts and the borders
of society? It is not so much because we will evangelize them,
but rather we will open ourselves to being evangelized by them."
(Pastoral Letter, 2015). The young people I taught also taught me
much, and they helped me to discover many forms of poverty.

Attention to the presence of God has led me to live two
kinds of experiences, one on a daily basis and the other during
life's high points. On a day-to-day basis and according to De La
Salle's model, it is mainly in my relationships with young people,
with the Brothers, and with all those who cross my path, that I
was led to refer to God as a source of light and strength, which
brought me to be attentive and available to others. Young people
who came to see me in the office would first ask questions about
the course or about an assignment, but often this was followed
by questions about their personal problems. I came to notice that

Someone was allowing them to find their answers themselves; I saw the intervention of the Holy Spirit. This is what gave meaning to my work as a teacher and educator.

Then there are significant times that allow for an even deeper awareness of the presence of God. Every day, the encounter with Jesus in prayer, Mass, and Communion constitutes the heart of my day and the source of true life. It is a radiant and strengthening presence that gives light and peace.

Other exceptional events bring even deeper experiences of God's action, such as my involvement in the 2014 General Chapter. I was and am still convinced that the Holy Spirit was present and at work throughout our discussions and deliberations in the 2014 General Chapter, especially in the revision of the *Rule*. Some seemed reticent throughout the process, though well prepared by the *ad hoc* committee. As the proceedings of the plenary sessions progressed, specific clarifications removed certain resistances or hesitations, and approval of the overall revision of the *Rule* garnered general consent. Where does this general agreement of minds and hearts come from, if not from the Breath that is also Light? An unforgettable experience.

Attention to the presence of God, which is a fundamental component of the spirituality of De La Salle, is a luminous path that is accessible to everyone.

Brother Fernando Lambert, FSC
District of Francophone Canada

God's Plans

I have had the privilege of teaching a student multiple times only rarely. Jokingly, I have referred to these students who knew me too well as my "Two-" or "Three-Time Losers." Luckily, nobody has ever had to endure me more than three times!

Among the first of my three-timers was a wonderful young woman—I'll call her Grace—who enrolled at an odd time in her freshman year of high school and was assigned to one of my English 1 sections. Her family had just moved into the area from out of state. Unlike her very quiet and reluctant older brother, who was placed in one of my sophomore religion sections, Grace was a vibrant, smiling, and hardworking student. I was delighted when she appeared in one of my sophomore religion classes the next year. She made friends easily, enjoyed her studies, and demonstrated all of the right qualities that teachers hope for in their students.

Grace's third encounter with me was in a senior English class. I noted early on in the class that she seemed uncharacteristically subdued. Since her school work continued to be good, I was not overly concerned, but I was aware that something had changed in her. I soon discovered why through the most tragic of circumstances.

One morning there had been a major accident involving a large truck and a car on a roadway not far from our school. Within hours, we learned that Grace had been riding to school with her stepfather that morning. He had been killed instantly in the accident, while she had been removed from the wreckage with only minor injuries. Understandably, she missed several weeks of school. The administration, counselors, and teachers were all determined to make her return to school as supportive as possible.

The first conversation Grace and I had on her return was businesslike. She wanted to know what work she had to make up and what timeline I expected of her to do it. Not surprisingly, she met her deadlines. But one afternoon, Grace appeared at my door asking to see me. I sensed instinctively that this was not about makeup work.

I can still see her face: serious, weary, and distant. "Brother John, I wish I knew why things turned out the way they did." I told her that I really didn't know why. Then she related how her life had turned since she had been the enthusiastic sophomore whom I remembered so well. Her family had moved here because her parents were not getting along. They had divorced and her mother had quickly remarried. Her new stepfather had been trying his best to make things right with the kids, including being helpful to Grace by driving her to school rather than have her wait for the school bus. Then they had the horrible accident.

"Why did he die and I didn't?" The best insight I had at the moment was to say, "Grace, maybe God has plans for your future that were not meant to end in that car that morning." Immediately, I felt that sinking sensation that my answer was trite and pious. How could that response possibly comfort or assist this wonderful and hurting young woman deal with this tragic turn in her life? Grace waited a few moments, and I am convinced I glimpsed just a hint of her smile, even through a few tears. "Thank you," she whispered, "It helps me to know that maybe God does have a special reason for me to live."

More than 30 years have passed since that day. I must honestly admit that I do not know what happened in Grace's life after her graduation. Yet, I believe that she experienced a special awareness of God being present to her in that awkward moment. God was present to both of us in that classroom. God had been present to her even in that crushed car. God, I trust, continues to be present to her wherever she may be today. That marvelous "Three-Time Loser" is accomplishing things that God could not do without her. And this graced teacher of marvelous losers has never forgotten how profoundly aware I have been since that very day that we are always and everywhere in the holy presence of our good God.

Brother John M. Crawford, FSC
La Salle University, Philadelphia, PA

There Is Life Under There

I walked my five-year-old son to the park the other day. As Timmy began playing in the pebbles that cover the ground, I took a seat on a low cement wall. My attention immediately turned to troublesome thoughts and responsibilities.

Timmy finished making a mound of pebbles and called out that it was a present for me. I wasn't interested. I had had a long day at work, and I wanted to relax a little. Surely I'm allowed to do that, right? Timmy continued to call for my attention, but instead I took my phone out to thumb through Facebook for the third time in 20 minutes.

"Daddy!" he said again. I put away my phone and mustered up some patience, "Yes, Timmy, what can I do for you?" "I made you a present," he said with a big toothy grin, forgiving me for my lack of attention. I walked over to the mound of pebbles and said, "Thank you so much, Timmy." "Open it!" he said excitedly. I moved the pebbles aside and found a dandelion inside. "Wow, thanks. This is awesome." I mustered as much enthusiasm as I could.

"There is life under there!" he said.

That is when I saw the big picture. Timmy wanted to share life with me! He wanted nothing more than to connect with me. He didn't know how, so he made something up. He extended his expression of love in the only way he knew how, and he did it without hesitation or fear of judgment. I, however, was trapped in my cave of inner thoughts, mindless and meaningless, thinking only of myself and how others should treat me. Timmy brought me into the present moment; it is only in the present moment that we find Life. Timmy taught me that God's presence is found in God's present (moment).

God is found in the sweetness of a strawberry and in the sorrow of a loved one passing away. God is found in the rose blooming at your feet and in the cloud passing above your head. God is present in all things. The thoughts of the mind are your creation.

How often do we sacrifice the beauty of the moment in front of us and squander our attention on anxious "what-ifs" or angry "I-can't-believe-they-said-thats."

Let's be clear. Worrying is not love, anger is not righteousness, and fear is not prudence.

For God's sake, let's get out of our minds and come to our senses! Life is lived with God in the present moment. And as it turns out, the present moment is all that we have. Sanctify the moment with a shower of attention. Sacrifice the worries of the future and the hurts from the past, because they are the toll that we pay to enter the garden of the present moment, because the beauty of this moment is more than just a nice thing. It IS the presence of God.

Peter Augros
Mullen High School, Denver, CO

Press On!

In my 18 years of teaching in a Lasallian school, I have come to treasure the grace-filled acknowledgment that begins our focus on intentional prayer. "Let us remember that we are in the holy presence of God" is an invitation, an exhortation, and a celebration of the many and varied ways that we experience the reality of God acting in our everyday lives.

In the fall of 2014, a Totino-Grace High School student died after suffering from brain cancer that she'd had since she was in second grade. Rachel is the closest I have ever come to being in the presence of a saint. She was positive, thoughtful, strong, never complained, and reminded us in word and deed that "every day is a gift." On a Friday in late September that year, Rachel died.

The next day our soccer team was scheduled to play a game. As I prayerfully drove to school, I wondered what to say to the 18 guys who were mourning the loss of Rachel. A car zoomed by on the highway, and its license plate simply read "PRESS ON." It wasn't just a nudge to keep going. "Press On" epitomized Rachel's fortitude and resilience. In the locker room, it is what I wrote on the board after acknowledging that today wasn't about soccer. Today was about loving and remembering Rachel. Before the game, we played Rachel's favorite song: "Somewhere Over the Rainbow." I don't remember too many details about the game, but I remember the sadness of the boys as they reflected on the impact that Rachel had had on each of our lives.

Later that day I received this email from one of our players: "I just want to share quite an amazing story with you. Today after the game, Jeff and I went to Chipotle for a post-game meal. Jeff was wearing his Rachel shirt so the man behind us in line asked about it. We went on to tell him what happened and the summary of it all and how she affected our community in such an amazing way and everything like that. He, of course, had his sincere condolences and wished us the best. Right before we ordered our food, we thanked him and started to turn around. His closing statement was, 'Press on boys, press on.' The world has amazing ways of doing things doesn't it? My new motto for all tough times is officially 'Press on!'"

"Let us remember that we are in the holy presence of God" manifests itself in large and small ways. This autumn day, as our community was grieving the death of our angel, our saint Rachel, we were reminded through God's grace that our journey to Jesus, our participation in the paschal mystery, is always pressing on with faith and zeal.

Bill Vance
Totino-Grace High School, Fridley, MN

We See God Very Well

Where is God? God is everywhere. If God is everywhere, why do we not see him? Because God is a pure spirit and cannot be seen by the eyes of the body. These are catechism questions and answers that we learned by heart as young people. It took us a lifetime to understand their meaning.

I am of the '70s generation of school youth. On Sundays we went to Mass without really understanding the meaning, but during the school week pastoral ministers helped us live significant moments with the intentional purpose of helping us live the experience of God. The goal of pastoral ministry at that time was to be a laboratory of faith.

After a weeklong summer experience in a Christian formation camp run by the Brothers, I was inspired enough to become a camp counselor. The deep experiences that we provided for young people allowed me to be a privileged witness to seeing the action of God in their hearts, and to detect its active presence. Though I had never heard the phrase, "Let us remember that we are in the holy presence of God," I had a deep intuition about it. The awareness of God's dynamic presence encouraged me to become more involved in touching the hearts of young people.

At the Collège Marie-Victorin, Brother Donald taught us that we could meet God in seven different ways: Mass, Scripture, sacraments, prayer, miracles, saints, and other people around us. This is what led me into the world of education, because this is where young people become the presence of the living God for me.

It is in educational settings where God's grace came to me: in a student who, in the process of catching up, finally understands the subject taught; in a young person with learning difficulties who regains confidence; in a student who takes up a challenge thought to be beyond personal capacities; in a young person who decides to make the service of others a passion and occupation; and in a colleague who comes to see a particular young person in a new way.

I also intensely lived the presence of God at the 43rd General Chapter in Rome in 2000, to which I was invited, along with other lay consultants. During that time, the questions seemed more numerous than the answers. And among the most piercing questions were those about how to live Shared Mission together today, how to respond better to our mission of human and Christian education, and how to do all this while respecting our respective identities. In spite of sometimes painful exchanges, everyone felt that the Holy Spirit was with us, present and active. This resulted in strong and bold directions and recommendations. I came back completely transformed.

Where is God? God is everywhere. If God is everywhere, why do we not see God? On the contrary, we see God very well!

Denis de Villers
District of Francophone Canada

The Power of the Eucharist

The Eucharist and interior prayer have been the bedrock of Lasallian prayer life. My early training was that the *Explanation of the Method of Interior Prayer* was a how-to guide for the uninitiated. As one matured, interior prayer became meditation. The Eucharist was the daily remembrance of the passion, death, and resurrection of Jesus that connected us together, allowing the Holy Spirit into our minds and our hearts at the start of each day. There was purpose. There was a relationship. There was an invigoration of the daily commitment to live a life of faithful service, not only to our vows, but also to our baptismal obligation to live a life of virtue. As I got older, I was able to perceive just how the fulfillment of these obligations altered how I lived and how God began to work through me. I experienced the power of God increasingly present in what I did.

Relying on the grace of the Holy Spirit, I was the founder of two Lasallian middle schools. I was keenly aware of what a dangerous time the transition from child to young adult could be. Anger and pain from unpleasant childhood experiences often manifested themselves as a lashing out at others or being directed inward as self-destructive behavior. If there is no healing environment within the culture of a school, there is little growth and much less happiness. Darkness descends, slowly and inexorably.

A seventh-grade boy, angry—no, furious—at his father's abandonment of him and his mother, took it out on all of us. He was rude, nasty, disrespectful, and purposely hurtful to his peers and the faculty. After several interventions with him, and confronting him about the harm he was doing to others, it was becoming time for him to walk away from the school community. He was in clear violation of our "Elements of Community" and our contract in the Code of Conduct. A thought came to me at Mass one morning: that this was a spiritual crisis. I knew that the most powerful tool I had available to help him heal was the Eucharist. So, in order for him to stay in the school, he had to join me at Mass every morning. He agreed.

I witnessed firsthand the great power of the Eucharist for him, beginning the process of letting in the Holy Spirit and coming to terms with his anger and his lashing out. It didn't take long for people to notice a change in how he conducted himself and how he began to reach out to people. On his own, he began to apologize to the people he had gone out of his way to hurt and humiliate. Each day, when he sat next to me at Mass, my prayer was for him and in gratitude for his being open to the power of the Spirit. He remained faithful to his promise. He grew in wisdom, age, and grace.

A week before graduation he asked me if we could get together to talk. He wanted to thank me for sticking with him and for not giving up. I told him just how proud I was of him for letting Jesus in to start the process of healing. As we stood up, he put his arms around me, buried his head in my chest, and sobbed. I admit that I got a little teary-eyed. I experienced, all the more deeply, the power of the Eucharist to nurture and to heal people.

We are good friends to this day. Apparently he told this story to his wife, because she has on several occasions thanked me for helping him. I always, always defer to the action and power of the Eucharist. Together, Jesus continues to live in our hearts!

Brother Brian Carty, FSC
De La Salle Academy, New York, NY

The Students
Continue to Teach Me

It was dark in the De La Salle Chapel. Fourteen hours earlier, this summer school class had met in the same chapel for the 6:00 a.m. Mass. The sun had been shining at that time, and a full day of "when I was hungry . . . thirsty . . . naked . . . a stranger" awaited the students.

Now the day was almost over, and the only light in the chapel came from a single candle embossed with the phrase: "Remember We Are in the Holy Presence of God." Everyone was tired, most were touched by what had happened that day, some were sharing. As their teacher for this 24-hour immersion class on urban poverty, I was inspired by their resilience. It was time for the teacher to become the student. What would they teach me? What would the teacher learn from the students?

I started the evening prayer service by asking, "Where did you meet Jesus today?" Was it on the city buses that took us from place to place? Did you see him on the other side of the serving line at the soup kitchen? Did you see him in the faces of the people you prepared lunch for with your own money at the homeless shelter? Was it at Catholic Charities, when you helped that lady take her food to the car? Maybe you found him when you toured the local homeless shelter and heard the man tell his story of clawing his way back to dignity from drug abuse, divorce, and unemployment. My students started teaching me where I can find Jesus.

"I found Jesus at the bus station. While we were sitting around waiting on our bus, I noticed people that were in need putting others' needs before their own."

"I saw him in my classmates' smiles and extra efforts."

"He was in the supervisor of the soup kitchen, who does this every day with a smile."

"I saw him in the lady at Iron Gate [Soup Kitchen] when she gave me a napkin with all her favorite Bible verses on it."

"I saw him at the bus depot in the son of the woman who shared her music with us."

"I found Jesus in the people eating at the Iron Gate Soup Kitchen. Having the opportunity to see so many unfortunate people was an amazing experience. I saw so many people that were so thankful and happy that we were serving them, even in spite of their situation; just like Jesus on the cross."

As this day ended, I knew that before the summer class was over, these young people would have similar reflections when we left a prison, an immigration center, a mosque, a mental health clinic, and a small Baptist church where the minister would share his stories of racism growing up black in America.

I also knew that my students would continue to teach me that "we are always and everywhere in the holy presence of God."

Ken Coughlin
Bishop Kelley High School, Tulsa, OK

A Shock, a Connection, a Memory

I was sitting in the back of the classroom. The class was Presentation Skills for Business, and it was near the end of the term. One of the young men, Rob, was ready to give the speech he had written for the persuasive argument assignment. This was usually a difficult speech for undergraduates, since it called for a reasoned argument and a certain level of emotional engagement.

Rob had just started speaking when another classmate, Nate, stood up, came over to me, said he had to leave, and then left. I was concerned, and somewhat annoyed. There was a rule in the class that no one was to disrupt things while someone was speaking. The speeches were videotaped and timed, and sometimes an interruption would completely derail a presentation.

When the class was over, I didn't get a chance to talk to anyone. But when I returned to my office, I wrote to both Rob and Nate. I wanted to commend Rob on his ability to hold things together and finish his speech, and I wanted to check on Nate. Nate was a very good student, so his behavior was unusual. I asked that each of them stop by my office during office hours the next day.

When they arrived, they arrived together. That was when I was told the whole story. The speech had been on the topic of drunk driving. Rob had started his speech with a photo of a mangled car. The car had had five high school students in it when it was hit by a drunk driver, and four of the young men were killed. The fifth young man in that car had been Nate.

The night before, Rob went looking for Nate in order to make sure that he was ok, because while he was delivering his speech, he saw that something had shocked Nate, and he just wanted to check in on him. Rob had no idea that the photo he had chosen, in order to startle the class into listening to him, was a snapshot of one of the worst days in Nate's life.

Rob had felt compelled to go and see a classmate whose reaction to the beginning of the speech had been so unexpected. As they sat and talked, they both had a chance to truly see one another. They had each been on campus for three semesters, and they had spent almost three months in my class. But they were very different types of men, and they were involved in very different activities. Rob was gregarious and in a fraternity, while Nate was shy and studious. But on that night, at God's prompting, they talked. As they spoke, Nate saw that keeping this tragedy a secret was not healthy, and Rob saw that he needed to be more aware of those around him.

When they finally came to my office, God had already done his work. He had helped two people move toward more mature and considerate versions of themselves, owning their blessings along with their flaws.

Over the years, I have seen God in our midst many times, such as the feeling of awe and reverence when one of our Muslim students started our Commencement Mass with a call to prayer, or the echo of a large group of Lasallians as we prayed in the Brothers' chapel in Rome at the end of the International Assembly in 2006.

But this one memory about Nate and Rob keeps bubbling to the top. It was a quiet moment, one that slightly altered the course of two young men's lives. But it reminds me that God is always there, trying to help us do the right thing. We just have to listen.

Marianne Salmon Gauss
La Salle University, Philadelphia, PA

Through the Innocence of Children

"Preach by your example, and practice before their eyes what you wish to convince them to believe and to do." (Med. 100.2)

I know that my life's mission is to become an ember of love for the young. This is God's way of igniting in the children the fire of faith.

I was about to meet a student in a counseling session. He lived with his mother, and he was suffering from the death of a close friend. I prayed to God that I would find the right words to say, but I wasn't sure where to begin.

I greeted Jose with a smile and a warm, "How are you doing?" He assured me that he was fine. I attempted to make a connection by asking him what he thought of the approaching snowstorm. Without hesitation, he responded, "You know, Mr. Regan, I worry about the people who have no place to live. There are kids my age who have no heat and no food. Other families have no money. What's going to happen to them? Who will help them?"

I did not know what to say. I was the one who wanted to comfort Jose and assure him of God's protecting presence in his life. But it was the words that he spoke and the love that he expressed with his words that filled our small meeting place with the abundant presence of God.

His example had touched my heart. He reminded me that forgetting oneself in the care for others is the way of God's protecting presence in our world.

I have always believed that God's loving presence is especially visible in the lives of children. I witnessed this holy truth once again as God blessed me with the truth of the Gospel, delivered through the priceless innocence of a child.

Kevin Regan
The San Miguel School of Providence,
Providence, RI

A Miracle Behind the Hair

We had a summer school program for our newest below-grade-level students. Summer school was a time to determine if the students could handle our college prep curriculum. Students had to pass summer school in order to be officially accepted. Summer was for weeding out those who just couldn't handle it.

One summer, along came Charlie. He had long, stringy hair that hung over his entire face. He sat himself as far away from me as he possibly could, and he proceeded to make himself invisible behind that hair.

I started my summer school class as usual, with a placement test that bottomed out at the fifth-grade level. Charlie bottomed out. In looking over his work, I couldn't believe the mistakes that he had made. He didn't appear to understand anything. How could we possibly bring this kid up four or more grade levels by the sophomore year, which was one of the requirements for legitimately accepting struggling students, since otherwise they would never be able to graduate?

And so I tried to help him throughout that summer. He never voluntarily raised his hand or asked for help. For the entire summer, he would only communicate monosyllabically and only when forced. I forced him often.

My colleagues and I met together at the end of the summer in order to discuss who we would accept. Charlie wasn't on any of our lists. Our director told us that Charlie's parents were begging us to take him. They were concerned about what would happen to him at his neighborhood school. We all strongly felt that he probably wouldn't make it in our college prep curriculum, but we didn't have the heart to turn him away. We accepted him, but with a cloud of doom over our heads. After all, what did they expect from us, a miracle?

The school year started, and in came Charlie's hair, with him somewhere behind it. He sat himself down in the back of the classroom again. And I kept forcing him. Slowly, day by day, I could see a little more of Charlie's face. Finally, one day, he raised his hand to answer a question. When I told him that he was correct, his arms shot up in the air, and he shouted, "Yes!!!" I nearly cried.

From that moment on, Charlie started coming around. He worked hard, came in for help, took notes, studied, and filled the holes in his math toolbox. One day, he came to school with his hair cut short. You could see the transformation in his step. He was simply blooming. Because he did so well, by the end of freshman year I was able to put him into the Algebra 1 class for his sophomore year. He finished the year with a B. I don't know what any of us expected, but what we got was a miracle.

When I think of how we came so close to saying "No" to Charlie, my heart breaks. How many other students could have bloomed if given the chance?

Thanks to Charlie and others like him, we no longer use summer school to weed out students. We accept them all without condition, and we use summer school to begin their Lasallian journey. We meet them where they are and help them become their best selves.

I think the Founder would approve.

Lorie Frias
Christian Brothers High School,
Sacramento, CA

The Bouncing Ball

Adults in our community have the opportunity to attend meetings at our Rhode Island Lasallian Group (RILAG) every couple of months. One night we were shown a video on the conditions of some of the Lasallian Kenyan schools with which we are twinned. Although the children there appeared to be very happy, there were greatly overcrowded living conditions and classrooms in need of repair. It brought me to tears.

As the twinning coordinator for our school, La Salle Academy in Providence, Rhode Island, I felt that traveling there would be a great learning experience for some of our students and that we could help the Kenyan students at the same time. After a year of preparations, our school nurse—who was as touched as I was by the movie—joined my husband and me as we began our journey. Five students were chosen, based on an essay contest about why they wanted to attend, and we all met at Boston's Logan Airport.

One of the students, Kyron, a keen basketball player, came to the airport bouncing a basketball. I thought, "Surely, he's not bringing that with us!" He told us that he takes it with him everywhere, and so I reluctantly agreed. But that ball cost us a delay at airport security of at least 15 minutes, because it was X-rayed and then the subject of TSA debate, because they thought that something might be smuggled in there. Finally, however, they allowed it onto the plane, and we were on our way to Nairobi.

We stayed with the Brothers at their Novitiate and at several of the Lasallian schools in Kenya. When we got to the first school, the children were playing basketball with a ball that was very old and ragged. It resembled a big ball of newspaper. To our great surprise, when Kyron saw this, he immediately gave his prized basketball to them and told them to keep it.

It was a time when the student taught the teacher. That the Holy Spirit could work through our passionate basketball player, without any prompting from an adult, was a great lesson.

There were many moving and touching moments during our trip to Kenya, and we were able to raise much-needed funds for the schools. But it all started when that ball—which I had thought was an annoyance—became a beacon of what it means to be Christian. We will never forget all of the lessons that we learned during that mission trip, and the experiences stay vividly with me to this day. But it all started with the bouncing of a ball.

I'm reminded of De La Salle's words: "Do your part to establish and to maintain the kingdom of God in the hearts of your students." (Med. 67.1) In this instance, my student's heart spread Christ's kingdom better than I ever could.

Leslie V. Martinelli
La Salle Academy, Providence, RI

God's Presence
in Moments of Grief

In 40 years of education, nothing touches me more profoundly than the death of a student, when suicide, violence, cancer, accidents, drugs, or physical challenges have shortened a life with so much potential. I can recall quite vividly the circumstances, pain, and sorrow of each death. At that moment, words of comfort to the family do little to ease the pain. As Catholics, we gather in prayer not so much to make sense of the situation as to be with one another in our quest for consolation.

At Christian Brothers High School in Memphis, Tennessee, in 1966, the members of the school band constructed a beautiful memorial garden after the death of the band president, who was killed in an automobile accident a few weeks before graduation. The school was completing its first year on the Walnut Grove Road campus. Once an undeveloped part of the property, the young oak trees planted in 1966 are now majestic sources of shade and beauty. Over the years, the name of each individual who has died while a student at CBHS has been added to the garden.

I have stayed in contact with many of the parents who have grieved over the loss of their child. They will remind me of my visit to the hospital, morgue, funeral home, or house—a message where presence, not words, provided some sort of comfort. I am inspired by their continued faith, which in many cases has only strengthened through the years. They have learned to live with their pain, to smile again, and to reach out to others who have experienced a similar tragedy.

Saint John Baptist de La Salle calls us to be ambassadors and ministers of Jesus Christ. Over the years, it has become much clearer to me how many colleagues, friends, parents, and, yes, even students, feel that same call.

The parents who maintained their faith through periods of grief offer hope in times of despair. As a Brother, I have come to realize that we are on this journey of life together. We are partners with one another. "Let us remember that we are in the holy presence of God," an invocation I have used thousands of times, provides guidance in everything that I do throughout any given day. Just as I believe that God has placed me in certain situations at any given time for a certain purpose, I also believe that God has placed others in my life as Brothers, mentors, and companions for the journey.

Brother Chris Englert, FSC
Christian Brothers High School,
Memphis, TN

Let Us Be Attentive!

An Inviting Presence

My Lasallian experience began when I was a student; but my commitment as an "actor" in the Lasallian mission began when I needed to work to pay for my studies. I first got a job as a supervisor in a boarding school and then as a young teacher in my own former school. Working at that time side by side with adults, I could sense the profound inspiration and zeal of many of my colleagues, Brothers and lay, teachers and educators. Their vibrant but discreet faith revealed to me the presence of God in their lives and prompted me to reflect on my own faith. What could the Lord be calling me to do? I decided to make a private retreat in a Cistercian monastery. During this blessed time and while in silent prayer for an extended period, I became convinced that he was calling me to the consecrated life of the Brothers, and I then decided to begin the necessary process of discernment.

Yes, at this decisive moment in my life, as in others later, I felt that God was present and calling me. He called me in complete freedom. This calling, rooted in my heart, would forge a conviction and lead to a commitment.

A Guiding Presence

Today, after years as a Brother of the Christian Schools, I understand the presence of God more as "the will of God in my regard," to repeat the last words of John Baptist de La Salle. The way God guides is discreet and efficacious. Like other Christians, I believe in his presence in the sacraments of the Church. But I sense it in a more direct way when his Word in Scripture comes at the right moment to encourage me in happy times and to lift me up in times of trial. God has also been present in the works of mission entrusted to me.

The Presence of God on Our Faces and in Our Silences

I have recognized the presence of God in the hearts of confreres, faithful friends, and colleagues who serve youth. It is an active presence even if it is not always mentioned by name. I have also recognized this presence in those youth who open themselves to the Word of life and are transformed by it.

Yes, in the shared works in our mission of education I have felt the presence of God: in our faces, in our smiles, in our joys and our sorrows, and also in our silences.

God for Us, God in Us, God among Us

"Let us be attentive!" This is a call often repeated in the Orthodox Liturgy. God is always present. If we remember his holy presence, it is precisely because he is always there. We are the ones who need to become attentive. For then, we recognize his mercy for us, the action of his Spirit in us, and his loving presence among us!

Brother Claude Reinhardt, FSC
District of France

In the Light of the Setting Sun

A participant of the Buttimer Institute of Lasallian Studies from 2002 to 2005, I cherished sitting in the chapel at Saint Mary's College of California, a sacred place that drew the community together at the end of each day. Shadows embraced the disparate congregation seeking the Light of the World by many pathways. This seeker always chose a middle-aisle pew, anticipating the nightly majestic arrival of the ever-so-slow, but always predictable, setting of the sun. Soft golden rays seemed like beacons of God's presence. They drew me into prayer as one of many wayfarers building the Kingdom of God, confident that God's work is truly our own.

The glory of it all is incalculable. Yet so often I take the predictability of the quotidian for granted. But Saint Mary's chapel is, for me, what the Celts would call a "thin place" where the presence of God is palpable, as One who loves me more than I can ever imagine. Yes, "Terrible is this place," I think, recalling the opening words of the Introit for the *Mass of Dedication of a Church*.

Nestled in the northern California hills, the open chapel doors gratefully receive the setting sun, its light signaling God's presence to the expectant silence of a Lasallian community, the gathering of disciples of Saint John Baptist de La Salle. I see us following him step by step—Catholics, Protestants, Jews, Muslims, Buddhists, and Atheists, among others—from the United States and from across the Lasallian world, lay educators walking together and by association with the Brothers of De La Salle, spreading the good news of God's love for all, but especially for the young and the poor. Our Lasallian mission is the salvation of students both in this world and in the next. We offer a practical education whereby students will make God's work in this world truly their own, as co-creators of an unfinished universe. Herein lies their path to salvation in the next world.

As I write these reflections on the words and deeds of the global Lasallian world, I am filled with gratitude to Saint John Baptist de La Salle and his followers, who have brought his vision of Christian education into accord with the signs of the times. My single act of gratitude becomes an endless chain of thanksgivings for relationships and for association in community. I realize that I stand on the shoulders of giants, that I am arm in arm with tens of thousands who "live Lasallian," and that I am one with the communion of Lasallians who have gone before me. How humble and how grateful I feel as I remember those many evening prayers at the Buttimer Institute and the contribution they made to my own spiritual journey to the new Jerusalem, where to borrow the words from Josef Locke's "The Holy City," there is "no need of moon or stars by night, or sun to shine by day."

John R. Wilcox
Manhattan College, Bronx, NY

Treated as if I Belonged

The first time I walked through the halls of a Lasallian school, it had been eight years since my last teaching experience. After many years of working in parish ministry, I was living in Denver, Colorado, and returning to the classroom as a high school theology teacher.

Making the decision to leave parish ministry and return to teaching was difficult. I was comfortable with my role and surrounded by people of faith who were also my friends. But the circumstances of my job and the gentle nudging of the Lord were inviting me to something new. At the time, I didn't know what a "Lasallian" school was, and I had never heard of Saint John Baptist de La Salle. I simply knew that there was a Catholic high school that needed a theology teacher, and that I was a person who needed a place to belong.

I was new to teaching high school students, and I was new to teaching theology. I could hardly find my way around the building and taught in several different rooms, so that I had to move each period like the students. I could remember only a few of my colleagues by name. I didn't even know who to ask for help. As I began my first day of school, I was afraid.

I was walking through the hall during a passing period with my arms full of papers, books, and supplies. The hall was crowded with students, and I wasn't sure how to find my next classroom. But I knew I had to hurry, because I needed to get there, set up, and be ready to teach as soon as the bell rang.

Preoccupied with all these worries, somehow my papers got away from me, scattering across the floor. I thought for sure that I would have to protect my things from students who would mindlessly walk all over them, that I might get knocked down while bending over in the crowd of students. Certainly they would be laughing at me.

But students I didn't know stopped and began picking up my things. Not only did they gather my things for me and ask me if I was all right, they offered to carry my things to my classroom. "Where can we take these for you, Ms. Niblack?" they asked.

These young men and women called me by name and treated me as if I belonged there. That was the moment that I knew I had found a home. It was my first glimpse of what it means to be a Lasallian inclusive community. Students I didn't know, knew me and were willing to go out of their way to take care of me, to help me, and to make me feel welcome. That was the moment that I knew how present God was to me, in bringing me to my new job—no, my vocation—as a Lasallian educator. I had found a home.

That one experience led me to develop an induction program at my school to welcome new teachers, so that other new teachers might also experience the holy presence of God through others.

Rita Niblack
Mullen High School, Denver, CO

An Unexpected Effect

I remember one day when I had to lead a community meeting about a very controversial subject, knowing that there was no unanimous agreement in the community. I was afraid of very heated exchanges, because there were Brothers who were in favor of the project that I would present, and others who were fiercely against it. My biggest fear was that some would come out of this encounter deeply hurt, due to their tendency to react passionately.

I was struck with the idea of starting the meeting by saying: "Let us remember, my Brothers, that we are in the holy presence of God." And so I did. The silence that followed surprised me. The invocation had an unexpected effect on the participants, because it had not been used for many years in this particular community. A short reflection followed, during which we voiced and recalled that God is present in the community as well as in each of its members.

The reminder of God's presence had a significant calming effect on the community. The exchanges took place in a climate of mutual trust. Everyone took time to listen to one another. Each comment was received as a gift that the speaker shared with the community. Even if one or another did not agree with a comment, he took the time to listen to the end, respecting the Brother who was speaking.

While we did not come to a final decision that pleased everyone, the important thing was that fraternal charity was safeguarded, that we were able to talk in a civilized way without insulting one another, all because God was really present at this meeting.

Since that time we have kept up the habit of starting each meeting with the invocation, "Let us remember that we are in the holy presence of God."

Brother Yvon Desormeaux, FSC
District of Francophone Canada

A Place of Refuge

Many years ago, I was working in one of Saint Gabriel's System's outpatient mental health facilities. Late one afternoon, a young man, a former client, entered looking for the therapist he had previously worked with. He explained that something bad had happened earlier in the day and that he was afraid. His therapist had told him in his final session that if he ever needed help in the future, he could come back. So, in his time of need, this young man did just that: he came back.

Unfortunately, his previous therapist was no longer with the agency. But luckily, in my role as director, I remembered him, and he remembered me. I invited him into my office to have a seat and a conversation about what was going on. He explained that things had been rocky lately between him and his girlfriend, and that earlier that afternoon, they had fought. His girlfriend, he said, had pulled a knife on him during the argument, and a physical altercation had ensued. While neither he nor his girlfriend was hurt, he fled when she called the police, and since he was already on probation, he was now concerned that the police were looking for him and that an arrest warrant had been issued. He didn't know what to do.

We talked for some time about remaining calm, and we considered all of the options. Finally, I was able to convince him that if he were to ever have a moment's peace, he would need to determine if the police were, in fact, looking for him. We decided together that I would call the police and ask them to send someone to my office, so that the situation could be safely and peacefully resolved. But I told him that before bringing police onto the premises, I wanted to make my boss aware. He said that was fine, as long as my boss wasn't Brother Dennis. Imagine my surprise! Brother Dennis was my boss, and coincidentally was the person this young man held responsible for "kicking him out" of one of our schools the previous year. My plan was unraveling, or so I thought. But when the young man thought about it for a moment, he sheepishly said, "Okay. You can tell him. Brother Dennis treated me fair."

I went upstairs and told Brother Dennis what was happening. His face lit up. He remembered the young man fondly and said, "I'll go sit with him while you call the police." When I returned to my office, Brother Dennis and the young man were reminiscing like two long-lost friends. We all sat together waiting for the police. The officers eventually arrived and confirmed that there was no warrant. To say that the young man was relieved is an understatement. After deciding that he would spend that night at his mother's house, the young man said his goodbyes, hugged Brother Dennis, and left with the officers, who were going to accompany him to his car (to make sure it had not been towed!).

I remember that day for two reasons. First, that young man's previous experience with our services had left him with a sense that Saint Gabe's was a sanctuary, a refuge, a safe place to which he could return for help. And second, I remember Brother Dennis's presence that day. He was eager to be with that young man, to accompany him through a troubling time, to ease his anxiety. Despite having been "kicked out" of school by Brother Dennis, the young man sensed his fairness and his compassion. Brother Dennis was that day (and remains), like so many other women and men of Saint Gabriel's System, an embodiment of God's holy presence.

James J. Black
Saint Gabriel's System, Philadelphia, PA

The Phone Call
That Changes Lives

O n what I assumed to be a very normal July day in Memphis, unexpectedly I received a phone call from a colleague that transformed this university in a most Lasallian way. The call was a request to help fund an outstanding Latino high school student who was not a citizen and could not qualify for any federal or state grants in spite of her outstanding high school record.

This call prompted me to call our director of admissions and ask how many other students like this student had applied to our university but could not qualify for any aid. The answer I received was startling . . . there were at least 10 students of high quality who could not afford an education with us because they were not citizens of the United States. The call to action was clear. How could I, as the president, find a way to educate these individuals, especially since there was no other way for them to receive an education in Memphis, given their immigration status? With my admissions director, we constructed a financial plan that required discounting tuition, creating a loan program, and most significantly, securing a multimillion dollar benefactor to support these students.

Unbelievably, when I mentioned our situation to a colleague, he responded supportively. Didn't he realize that my request was going to amount to several million dollars as the number of students who would qualify for such a program had now doubled to 20?

Between the time of that July phone call and the start of the semester in August, we enrolled 25 DACA (Deferred

Action for Childhood Arrivals) students into our programs. At the completion of their first year, 24 of them remained, and one had to leave to get married. These students not only performed in the classroom, but they also transformed our student life culture, creating an awareness of their own cultures and plight that helped inform our university's traditional college students.

The first cohort recently graduated, and several national philanthropic organizations have provided additional funds, enabling the number of Latino students on campus to grow to more than 150. Because of these new students, our campus has become much more Lasallian, as the holy presence of God has come to pervade so much more of what we do on a daily basis.

John Smarrelli
Christian Brothers University,
Memphis, TN

Touching a Young Heart
on a Flight

For me, the clarion call throughout the day, "Let Us Remember," provides an opportunity to personalize my belief in the resurrection. Each time I pause to "remember," I pray for greater clarity regarding the transformative insight of viewing the resurrected Jesus of Nazareth as the human face of God. For me, personalizing the resurrection helps change the way I conceptualize God. For me, "I have seen the Lord" has to become a personalized "seeing," a seeing of INSIGHT. It is an insight that God is truly present in whatever time zone I'm in, whatever manner of activity I am involved in, and whatever place I find myself.

When I served as the director of education for the legacy New Orleans-Santa Fe District, I was returning from an out-of-state meeting, and because of my accumulated bonus miles, I was flying first class. I was already settled in my seat when a small boy, with the assistance of the gentleman accompanying him, took the seat next to me. The boy was maybe eight or nine years old. Once the boy was settled in his seat, the gentleman left to take his seat in the coach section of the plane.

Although I continued to read whatever it was I was reading, in my peripheral vision I could not help but notice that the boy kept turning around, looking towards the back of the plane. He could not sit still. His body language more and more bespoke nervousness, fear, agitation, apprehension, and anxiety.

Saint La Salle, in his meditation for Pentecost Sunday, leaves no doubt as to why "Let Us Remember" is the indispensable, motivating mantra for what all Lasallians say and do, when he writes,

"You carry out a work that requires you to touch hearts, but this you cannot do except by the Spirit of God." (Med. 43.3)

I had a heart next to me that needed touching. So I caught the eye of the flight attendant. She came over, and I said, "Would you please check with the gentleman accompanying the boy sitting next to me, and see if he wants to trade places with me?" I got this deer-in-the-headlights look, and she said, "Would you please repeat what you just said?" I did, and she left to carry out my request, shaking her head.

The gentleman accepted my invitation. As I left to take my seat in the coach section of the plane, the joy and happiness radiating on the face of the young boy left me with a feeling that God was indeed present and residing in a heart that had been touched!

Brother David Sinitiere, FSC
District of San Francisco New Orleans

Recognize the Moment

Some people may think of being in God's holy presence as a large event or a life-changing moment in their lives. But God's presence can be found in the most simple, small interactions that happen every day; we simply don't see them all the time or are too "busy" to receive this gift.

At the beginning of my Lasallian teaching career, I had Mark in chemistry class. School came easily to him, which led to high success and a sense of achievement. One day, he came to me with a severe misunderstanding of a topic that we were working on in chemistry class. His demeanor was sheepish, vulnerable, and defeated as he asked me for help. He appeared ashamed that he couldn't grasp the subject. In that moment of need, I saw God's presence in Mark. As I helped him with the topic, I saw a great deal of pride and confidence come back to him. A few days later, he confided that his girlfriend had broken up with him, and that his parents were having relationship issues. These external distractors blocked his thinking and academic focus. That small conversation—seeing the vulnerability in him, and my being available to listen—helped me to know this as a graced moment of experiencing God's holy presence for both of us.

God's holy presence isn't just found in a student seeking out an adult. Richard, a two-year starter and all-conference football player, was having a tough time getting a jump start to his senior year, the most memorable and fascinating year in a young athlete's career. When I approached him about his drop in playing performance from the previous year, he divulged issues he was having with being a possible parent and how he was going to deal with these new stresses. I was aware of God's presence in this encounter, and that prompted me to engage Richard and try to figure out how I might best be of help. I also believe Richard was able to see God's presence in me, amidst all of the noise and extraneous stimuli of today's world, and thus be open to receive this gift of God's presence in another person, and discuss the trials and tribulations with which he was dealing. God's holy presence is one of the many gifts that are given to us many times a day. Our task is to recognize the moment and to be open to receive it.

Charles C. Dimovitz II
Christian Brothers College High School,
St. Louis, MO

Rituals of Remembering

My experience of the holy presence of God began in my family and continued throughout my ministry of more than 60 years in Québec and Cameroon. My mother, a country school teacher, lived constantly in the presence of God. Two passages of Holy Scripture guided her whole life: "Walk before me, and be blameless" (Gen 17:1) and "Those who love me will keep my word, and my Father will love them, and we will come to them and make our home with them" (Jn 14:23).

Everything was an invitation to recall the presence of God. Even at breakfast, while we, the children, attracted by the smell of pancakes copiously sprinkled with maple syrup, took our seats at the table, she would ask us: "When you got up, did you thank God for life? Did you offer your actions of the day?" Then everyone had to answer a question from the catechism, which she knew by heart. In the evening this same ritual, stripped of annoying preaching, reminded us of the presence of God.

During the summer, I often went from the house in order to bring cold drinks to the workers. Mama would then take the opportunity to say to me, "Have you thanked God for the beautiful sun? Your father will be able to gather a good harvest of alfalfa that the cows will appreciate this winter." Today, when I pray the *Song of the Three Young Men* (Dan 3:52–90), I regret that somewhere we don't find the words: "Alfalfa, clover and millet, bless the Lord."

A few years later, I was entrusted with my first class of sixth-grade kids. Every morning when I entered class, I bowed before the crucifix and then knelt to worship God present. One day a student asked me why I knelt down every day. After hearing my explanation, another student asked me, "Can we pray with you?" All year long this became a moment of daily grace.

In 1962, I was at Vogt College in Yaoiundé. From the first day of class I blessed the bell—it seemed as though I could hear my mother—that invited us to quiet recollection every hour and half hour. In each class, a student broke the silence by proclaiming, "Let us remember that we are in the holy presence of God." And all the students in chorus would answer, "Let us adore him." This wonderful ritual had so marked generations of students that at the first meeting of alumni, the president asked that we bring him the bell that rang the hours and half hours. At the end of the presentations he rang the bell and said the invocation that we all knew so well. At that very moment all the participants were silent; it was a long silence filled with a presence and wonderful memories. The teachers had won the hearts of their students . . . I tasted the fruits of the presence of God: a deep peace and great joy.

Brother André Dubuc, FSC
District of Francophone Canada

Sharing God's Splendor

Have you ever had one of those sacred moments that touched your heart and will stay with you forever? I have, and I owe this one to my two colleagues who were classmates at the Buttimer Institute of Lasallian Studies, held at Saint Mary's College in Moraga, California.

The three of us arrived at Buttimer and knew virtually no one else during the first year of our summer course. Although we were surrounded by wonderful colleagues from all over the country, there was just something about these two that made us fast friends. All three of us had a deep faith, and we loved our work in Lasallian ministries. We spent our weekends together, studying and rambling up and down the trails around the campus. Conversation was easy among us, as we shared stories of our childhoods, our lives, and our current work in Lasallian ministries.

Our little excursions allowed us moments of beauty and grace and laughter; for example, turning a corner and coming face-to-face with a fawn and her mother feeding beside the trail, or the time that John dramatically "saved" us from a snake, only to find out that it was a stick! We were blessed by our friendship, and by the third and last summer, our classmates referred to us as the three musketeers.

The final summer loomed, and we realized that we had not visited the famed Saint Mary's College Redwood Grove. So late one afternoon, we headed out to find it. We ambled down an unknown path that was dappled with late afternoon sunlight, our conversation flowing easily. As we found the grove of majestic redwood trees, our senses took over, and we breathed in the magnificent smell of the redwoods, craning our necks skyward as we marveled at the height of these majestic trees.

As we moved further into the middle of the grove, we discovered a statue of the Virgin Mary. It was neglected, so we took it upon ourselves to remove the leaves and cobwebs to leave her a little better than we had found her. As we admired our handiwork, one of the musketeers suggested we pray the Hail Mary in our three native tongues.

That moment, as the sun was low in the sky, surrounded by the quiet splendor of God's beauty, we prayed together in English, Spanish, and Gaelic our common prayer in honor of Our Lady. The experience touched us all so deeply that we couldn't speak for several minutes after it was over. We were awash with God's holy presence.

We left the grove, bonded in friendship, knowing full well that we had experienced God's holy presence that afternoon, and that Jesus was in our hearts, forever.

Maggie McCarty
Bethlehem University Foundation,
Beltsville, MD

God's Presence in a Father's Love

I learned of a freshman who had been diagnosed with leukemia after his eighth-grade graduation. He had missed a majority of his freshman year, and when he was able to come to school, he needed to remain on the first floor and work in the school library. He progressed, and it was thought that his cancer might be in remission. However, towards the end of the summer, the leukemia returned even more aggressively, and he returned to the hospital at the end of August. Jose required several rounds of chemotherapy, which played havoc on his 15-year-old frail body. The first round caused his body to break out in painful sores from head to toe. It was at this point that I had begun to visit Jose in the hospital with Brothers, school staff, and fellow classmates. I also began to truly experience and get to know this young man and his family. Truly, it was a family of faith who put their trust in God's providence.

The second round of chemotherapy left Jose unable to use his legs. He no longer had any feeling below his hips and would now be restricted to a wheelchair. There were days when he was extremely annoyed and grumpy, but most days he would be his tough self and talk about how much he missed school and wanted to return to be with his classmates. He was an honor student and very serious about his studies.

Miraculously, he overcame these treatments, persevered, and asked to return to school. On a cold day in February, he arrived at school with his dad in the family minivan. My schedule allowed me to assist with Jose's arrival and departure that day and in the days that followed. It became crystal clear to me that I was experiencing God's presence in a very practical and tangible way.

I would meet the minivan at the curb and assist Jose in exiting, preparing the wheelchair while his dad came around to the passenger door side. Dad would bend over, allowing Jose to clasp his hands around his father's neck so that he could be lifted into the wheelchair. The first time I witnessed this it took my breath away. I was witnessing the unconditional love a father has for a son, and witnessing God in my midst. The process was reversed at dismissal time.

The feeling that accompanied the experience did not subside in the least. I was moved in the same way each and every day for the remainder of the semester, many days with tears in my eyes. Jose persevered through the next five months, passing each of his three Regents exams in June.

In a letter to a Brother in May of 1701, Saint La Salle said, "The presence of God will be a great advantage to you to help and to inspire you to do your actions well." I felt blessed to be reminded of God's holy presence, alive on a side street in the Bronx each day for five months. It certainly has helped and inspired me in what I say and do.

Jose returned to the Lord on October 5, 2016. May he rest in peace!

Brother Richard Galvin, FSC
District of Eastern North America

More Than a Study Session

I absolutely love meeting with alumni of Saint Mary's University of Minnesota because they share great stories about their college experiences. Sometimes those stories depict memories of their time on athletic teams, humorous residence hall experiences, or friendships formed with classmates. In this example, an alum shared a meaningful experience with me over dinner one evening. Her story focused on a faculty member who took the time to teach her a lesson that she will never forget.

The professor, a De La Salle Christian Brother, taught physics. His student indicated that this was definitely not her favorite subject. In fact, she was only taking the class because she needed to fulfill the core requirement. Although it was her second attempt at the class, it was the first time that she took the class with this particular professor. Adding to her nervousness, she knew that she needed to finish the class with a passing grade, since graduation was only one week away.

Visiting with me, she recalled vividly how much anxiety she experienced while taking any exams. She would freeze up and forget everything she knew. Thankfully, this physics professor commonly offered study sessions before final exams. Hoping to improve her grade, she went to a session and—to her surprise—she was the only student who showed up.

The student told the Brother about her test anxiety. He said, "Let's do a few problems on the board." He asked her questions, and each time she would have to calculate the answer. This continued for two hours. Back and forth . . . a question and an answer, another question and another answer. At the end of the night the Brother asked the student how she thought the exam was going to go the next day. The student responded that although she thought the review had gone well, and she felt confident about knowing the information, she feared that during the exam she would once again freeze up, forget everything, and fail the class—which would ultimately lead to her not being able to graduate.

The Brother responded, "Don't worry; you just passed the exam. There is no need to come in for the final, because you just completed it. You passed the class." The student could not believe it.

Now a proud alum of the university for about 40 years, she was happy to share this story—a time in her life when someone showed her what the holy presence of God looked like. In that experience, the holy presence of God was seen in a professor, a person willing to take the time to assist a student who was struggling and who wanted so badly to succeed.

Tim Gossen
Saint Mary's University of Minnesota,
Winona, MN

43

Classroom Fears and Insights

Most of us Lasallians might recall our first years of teaching as mainly exercises in survival rather than the honing of one's craft; at least, that's what my first years were like. My number one fear was losing control of the class. I considered myself a sensitive guy, but there was no way that I was going to show the class the real me, for fear of them taking advantage of that sensitivity. My second fear was not knowing enough. What if a student asked me something that I didn't know? For some reason, saying "I don't know" didn't occur to me then. I would learn that answer a number of years later.

I began teaching high school religion to freshman boys in 1971, when textbooks had not yet caught up with the wisdom of Vatican II. In fact, those were years without any hardbound religion texts. I scrambled for materials, ones that included both the Bible as well as current genre resources like the musical *Jesus Christ Superstar.* (Don't tell my department chair!)

I coached immediately after school, returning to school in the evenings to teach songs for the school musical, *Hello, Dolly!* One night in the middle of the week, I went to bed without having prepared for the next day's classes. And I either forgot to set the alarm or didn't hear it, having intended to wake up early and prepare those classes. Therefore, I knew that on that day I would have to "wing it," and I dreaded going to class.

During my homeroom class, I came up with a few generic questions about an assigned reading that I had not yet read. Instead of our usual routine, I split the class into small groups, wrote the questions on the blackboard, and asked the students to come up with answers to the questions. I had never trusted them to be in small groups before this class and didn't quite know how all this would turn out.

I stood on the periphery policing the area, and I couldn't believe what I saw. The students began discussing the reading with one another. I didn't have to be at the center of the learning! (Yet another important lesson for me to learn.) Some of the groups started edging their chairs closer to one another so as not to be overheard by the other groups. All of a sudden it hit me. These 14-year-olds were enveloped in talking about Jesus! It sounds strange, I guess, but I was overcome—a huge lump in my throat, seeing their eyes meeting their fellow students' eyes. I can still see some of their faces. But there we were, in Room 17, whisked away from the ho-hum cinder blocks of tasks, and instead basking in the holy presence of God.

I had to turn away from them, worried that my fogged-up eyes would dare to drop a tear. Out of the blue, once I let go of control, God was there.

Brother Armand Alcazar, FSC
Christian Brothers of the Midwest

Bringing a Mosaic to Life

"So God created humankind in his image . . ."
—Gen 1:27

In a mosaic, the image becomes clearer as the pieces become smaller, but the smaller the pieces, the more pieces you need to realize the image.

Working at SECOLI (Lasallian International Cooperation Service) from 2003 to 2012, I traveled extensively in Africa and Asia. I have been blessed to meet thousands of people in 62 countries. I say blessed because I believe that we experience the presence of God in the people whom we encounter.

One of the countries that I visited was Vietnam. What would become of our Lasallian mission if we lost our schools? That is what happened to the Brothers in Vietnam. They lost their schools in the North when the French left in the 1950s. And when the Americans left in the 1970s, they lost their schools in the South.

When Saigon fell in 1975, one-third of the Vietnamese Brothers left their vocation as Brothers, one-third emigrated elsewhere as Brothers, and one-third remained as Brothers in Vietnam, some of them spending years in jail. The Brothers did retain some of their residences, however, even if they were on the roofs of confiscated schools. In time, the Brothers established houses of formation and catechetical centers, as well as centers for vocational training, student hostels, and informal education centers. It is even probable that the Brothers will eventually resume operating formal schools.

On a 2006 visit to Vietnam, I was invited to a dinner given by former students of the Brothers. Two "Old Boys" (alums), two other Brothers, and I set out for the restaurant. It was not until we arrived at the restaurant that I realized we were not simply a party of five. The restaurant was completely filled with more than 200 men and women who had been students of the Brothers over a period of more than 30 years.

There were glimpses of God everywhere, especially in the patience and persistence of the Vietnamese Brothers as they were overcoming serious obstacles, in the appreciation and faithfulness of their former students as shown in that gathering of former students, and in the promise and joy on the faces of the children that the Brothers are currently serving.

Anyone can find a piece of the image of God in the people they encounter, if they look for it. But if you meet enough people and glimpse their small reflections of God, your own image of God will become clearer, and the mosaic will come alive.

Brother Stephen Tuohy, FSC
Bethlehem University,
Bethlehem, Palestine

Touching the Educator's Heart

"Do you have faith that is able to touch
the hearts of your students
and to inspire them with the Christian spirit?
This is the greatest miracle you can perform
and the one that God asks of you,
for this is the purpose of your work."

(Med. 139.3)

Numerous "miracles" of God's shining bright presence took
place during my ministry at a residential treatment program
for court-committed juvenile delinquents. Breaking through the
tough exteriors of these hardened young men, whose lives were
damaged by drug and alcohol problems, abusive and negligent
families, and unbelievably horrible life stories and conditions, was
quite a challenge. The presence of God became apparent when
these students finally let down their defenses, allowing us to overcome their distrust and work through issues in their lives. Some
of these men are now living successful, happy lives. Unfortunately, others are dead or serving long prison sentences.

One "presence of God" event involved my youth care work
with Bill, a 14-year-old street urchin. Abandoned by his father
at an early age, Bill spent his days running the streets with his
buddies, only returning home at night to sleep. In addition to
stealing, truancy, and petty crimes, Bill was a regular "huffer." He
got high inhaling a dangerous chemical glue solvent. Bill was also
a "bedwetter" when he was with us. The remnants of the solvent
in his system were so powerful that we had to replace his mattress
after his urine ate through it. When high, "huffers" experience
an initial "rush" which makes them believe they are invincible.

On one occasion, after Bill failed to return from a home visit, we spotted and captured him on his usual corner. When I got him into our car, we found ourselves in an intense battle, since Bill had just inhaled the solvent and was so crazed by the fumes coursing through his brain.

In our residential setting, when he was not "high," Bill was friendly, gentle, and cooperative. Through daily interactions and regular counseling sessions, I was able to help Bill examine his painful life circumstances and self-destructive behaviors, including chemical abuse and child prostitution. While Bill was open in discussing his life and seemed genuinely interested in making necessary changes in his behavior, weekend home visits typically ended disastrously, with Bill returning to his previous behaviors.

While God's presence was evident throughout my efforts with Bill, my powerful "presence of God" moment happened months after Bill's release from our program. I experienced the receiving end of "touching hearts." While looking for another runaway in Bill's neighborhood, I was surrounded by a group of "huffers" who were unhappy that I had invaded their territory. As I searched for a route of escape, I heard a familiar voice happily exclaim, "Brother David, it's great to see you!" Bill gave me a big hug, then introduced me individually to his "huffer" buddies, explaining that I was a "special friend" who had helped him while he was put away.

I was genuinely moved by his welcome, display of affection, and appreciative words that day. My heart was definitely touched. I never saw Bill again. I learned recently that before he passed away, Bill dedicated his life to counseling and assisting the homeless and disenfranchised. May we be reunited in heaven one day.

Brother David Trichtinger, FSC
District of Eastern North America

Making a Difference

Some years ago I started working at Lewis University in Romeoville, Illinois, in the Office of Mission and Planning. It was a new venture for me, and I looked forward to the new experiences and challenges. Before the first semester was finished, the chair of the theology department asked me to consider teaching one section of the first-year course, Introduction to Christian Theology. While I had taught in high school for some years, this would be my first college teaching experience. I accepted and started the following semester.

Two challenges presented themselves almost immediately. The first was the apathy exhibited by some students, which surprised me, and the second was a couple of students who were evangelical Christians and would not accept the interpretation of the Bible that my Catholic education had given me. I worked on both areas for the entire semester. I must admit that several times I recalled De La Salle's thoughts that if he had known in the beginning what he was getting himself into, he would never have started.

Teaching the same course to a different set of students during my second semester started on a different tone. I was eager to get to know the students. They came from a variety of backgrounds and religions. One aviation major named Joseph was a Sikh and turned out to be the only student who earned an "A" for that semester. But what happened outside the classroom was more telling.

One day as I was walking across campus, I met Kathryn, who had been in my first-semester class. She was a Baptist, and we had some interesting discussions in class. She stopped me to say how grateful she was for my class and for the new insights that she had gained about Christianity. She said that she was inspired by the course, and in the new semester she had joined University Ministry as a peer minister, signed up for an evening Bible study, and was exploring various student service opportunities that University Ministry sponsored. She told me that my course had made a difference in her life, and she was grateful and also excited for the new opportunities that were now in front of her. As she thanked me, I had a vivid sense of the presence of God surrounding us.

When she started back across campus, I realized that in some small way I had touched her heart with the Christian Spirit, which De La Salle said was "the greatest miracle you can perform." (Med. 139.3) The experience confirmed for me another saying from De La Salle: God "has chosen you to do his work." (Med. 196.1)

Live Jesus in our hearts . . . Forever!

Brother Joseph Martin, FSC
Christian Brothers of the Midwest

Look, Listen, Love

The ride to the adult day care center was normal. The bus we rode on was an ordinary school bus. The students with us were ordinary kids—all crammed with extraordinary possibility. And we were to witness this in a real, concrete way.

We entered the building to letters and numbers being called out in both English and Spanish: B-11, N-35, O-70.

As a teacher, I was glad that our guys could work on their Spanish skills. But after "11" (in Spanish) was called and one of the residents joked audibly, "sounds like Beyoncé the singer," I knew this day was special.

I assigned each of our students to one resident of the home and encouraged them to sit with them as Martha's sister Mary had sat with Jesus in Luke's Gospel. "Look, listen, and love," I told our students. And Joshua did just that.

Veronica did not want to play any games, she just wanted to color at a table alone. When I left Joshua, the captain of the hockey team, with her, I thought to myself, "This is not going to go well."

When I came back to check in with them, Veronica knew all about Joshua's grades, hockey team, and girlfriend. Likewise, Joshua got an earful about her children, how Camden, New Jersey, used to be, and how much she enjoys playing Scrabble! He was so touched by his encounter with Veronica that he shares with everyone her stories and continues to show off the picture that she colored with him.

That evening at prayer, joy beamed from Joshua's smile as he shared how wonderful their conversation had been, leading me to believe that he experienced God that day.

Every day I say, "We are in the holy presence of God." But do I remember? Do I remember that we are in the holy presence of God? Do I recognize "Jesus beneath the poor rags of the children whom you have to instruct"? (Med. 96.3)

When we remember that we are in the holy presence of God, we are charged to be the holy presence of God to the world. When we remember, our eyes are open to God in our life. And when we remember, joy beams from our smiles as well.

For me, as a Lasallian educator, the easiest way to remember that we remain in the holy presence of God is simply to see the face of Jesus in the students entrusted to our care. To be in their extraordinary presence is to see, to feel, and to remember that God is with us always.

Christopher C. Panepinto
St. Joseph's Collegiate Institute,
Buffalo, NY

A Sudden Reminder

I had been teaching senior religion at Beckman Catholic High School, Dyersville, Iowa. Graduation day, 1976, found me with mixed emotions. I was leaving Beckman to become Auxiliary Visitor, reason enough to feel conflicted, since I dearly loved the students I was teaching and was aware that not only would the class of 1976 now be scattered elsewhere, but also that I would not be there for the next class of students. However, what was even more concerning was the immediate absence of Roy, one of the better students in the class. No one knew why he was not there, but his mother said he had left to hitchhike across the country. She did not know why and agreed that the decision appeared totally out of character for him. I left Dyersville, assuming I would probably never see or hear from Roy again.

However, on Christmas morning of that same year, I was visiting my parents, who lived near Dyersville, when I received a phone call from Roy. He asked if we could get together, and we arranged to meet in the parking lot at Beckman Catholic the following morning and then go somewhere for breakfast. Roy told me that he had freaked out at graduation time, hitchhiked across the country, gotten mixed up with drugs, engaged in other risky behaviors, never set foot in a church, and totally ignored his family, friends, and anything he had been taught by his parents or by Beckman Catholic.

In the fall he enrolled in a state university but said that he felt totally sad and disconnected from any reality. One day, while spacing out in one of his classes, the phrase, "Let us remember that we are in the holy presence of God" flashed through his mind. He said to himself, "Where did that come from?" He then recalled, "We said that every day in Brother Stephen's religion class." He said he spent the rest of the university class period mentally beating up on himself because he realized that since he had graduated from Beckman Catholic, he had not done one thing to remind himself that he is in the presence of God. He went on to say that, then and there, he committed himself to go to Mass every weekend from then on, or at least until he would find something else to remind him that he was in God's presence.

I again visited in the late 1980s and learned that Roy had gone on to get a degree in education and was teaching in a Catholic school in California, hopefully forever remembering that he lives in the holy presence of God. Roy's story has impacted me significantly, causing me to consistently repeat the powerful phrase, "Let us remember that we are in the holy presence of God," whenever I have led a prayer with students, colleagues, parishioners, youth groups, wedding and funeral dinner guests, families holding vigil when a loved one is dying, or with any individual or group open to pray with me.

Brother Stephen William Markham, FSC
Christian Brothers of the Midwest

Let Us Not Forget

"Let us remember that we are in the holy presence of God." It is in a state of awe and gratification that I ponder and reflect on the immense power this common invocation has for me, imagining the voices of Lasallians spreading across the oceans and mountains in different languages and indicating that we, all of us, in spite of our circumstances and situations, are in the holy presence of God. It is the invocation that connects and reconnects the Lasallian world within a common prayer.

"Let us remember . . ." —this comes across to me as meaning, "Let us not forget." It reminds me not to forget the protection and guidance of God that I have experienced in my life journey. It is this holy presence that I pause to recall as the invocation is pronounced. It is a moment of grace with gratitude, to remember the blessings experienced while pondering the joy of being in His holy presence in the here-and-now during the silence that follows the invocation.

The holy presence of God is something sought and felt as part of my apostolate, one where a religious person is revered and expected to give moral leadership. It is my experience, both as a teacher and an administrator of schools, that parents and students need such a place—a holy place, a person who helps them see beyond the ordinary, a community where they are treated with respect. In a questionnaire that we had sent to parents, one response was bold and clear about why these particular parents sent their children to our school: "There is something about this place, something about the tradition. Call it moral education or high expectation, but it is far deeper and more sacred than that. I believe I send my child to where God's presence is visible." And a Muslim parent responded: "Because of the habits and sense of respect that my son has learned at this Catholic school, I find it easier to teach him our faith."

I believe that we can experience the holy presence of God in the faces of the young that we serve if we ourselves strive to see everything with the eyes of faith. The more we practice the Lasallian core principles in our apostolate, the more the holy presence of God is felt. In teaching students who are deprived of basic needs—girls who run away from early marriages arranged by parents, and kids who do not get the support of their fathers—I came to learn what the presence of the Brothers and the provision of quality education could mean. For many of them, the presence of the Brothers is a sign of the holy presence of God within their situation.

For me, it is a continual reminder of the Spirit of Faith and God's providence that enables me and all of those who are part of the Lasallian mission to trust that in His presence extraordinary things do happen. It is a huge responsibility. It is not about my ego or intelligence, my doubts or enlightenment; it is about God and what He wants me to do in His sight.

The Scriptures tell us that in the presence of Jesus at Cana, ordinary water was changed into fine wine, and in His presence at the shore, professional fishermen whose nets were empty found them suddenly teeming with fish. Similarly, I believe that the vocation of Brothers bears its true meaning in the realization of God's holy presence in everything that we do.

Brother Belayneh Medhanit, FSC
Lwanga District of Africa

Strength in Quiet Attentive Presence

While with a truly "stretched out," uncontrollably angry, and inconsolable student, I eventually asked, "What is going on? What is pushing you to such anger?" He began to angrily spit forth his story of neglect, abuse, and emotional injury. Trying to listen as carefully as possible to understand and absorb the incredible hurt fueling his anger, I didn't know what to say so as to not sound trite, or diminish his pain. I realized with increasing consternation that I had no idea how to help this young man with his profound suffering.

Suddenly, I heard him spit at me, "You got nothing to say!?" Stunned, I sat quietly, then said tentatively, "I am digesting all that you shared. I see that this was not easy to share, especially with someone you hardly know. I am appreciating your trust in me by sharing your difficult experiences." "Really," he said. He then heaved forth another segment of deep painful suffering! My head spun in the face of such unbelievable harm and hurt, my sense of cluelessness increasing.

Suddenly and shockingly, I heard the young man say, "Thank you, Brother!" I stammered, "Thank you?" "Yes Brother," he said, and I will never forget the next words: "You are the first adult to ever hear me out." I was not sure what exactly he meant. He explained: "All adults, my parents, aunts and uncles, judges, probation officers, teachers and counselors, EVERYONE, just cuts me off and tells me what I should and should not do. 'Don't get upset' or 'calm down.' But you heard me out!"

The power of quiet attentive presence with active listening means not talking or reacting, but rather being responsive with silence, so that empathy and emotional resonance might well up. This is one form of the holy presence of God. So often we feel compelled to do or say something. A colleague at Saint Gabriel's Hall in Audubon, Pennsylvania, often said, "Just sit with them, walk with them, and suddenly you will see and hear something." The young man reaffirmed the "see and hear" principle of Quality Presence for me. Avoid the temptation to define the experience of others or to tell others how to feel. Holy presence is walking with another, and sitting in the spot where pain, joy, abandonment, bewilderment, or discovery is for another. It is beholding another. Connecting with another heals as one feels an increased sense of belonging, feeling beheld. This is my experience of the presence of God.

While in Africa, someone explained that a Swahili greeting begins with, "Where are you?" followed by "I am here," and ends with the return response, "I see you." I feel God sees me where I am. I, in turn, have the privileged opportunity to ask other persons, "Where are you?" And when he or she puts forth, "I am here," I then have the additional privilege of truly seeing them with my quality of presence, seeing and experiencing the presence of God with that other person!

Brother Brian Henderson, FSC
District of Eastern North America

An Authentic Experience for Students

O n the day before Thanksgiving, I was not thinking about the presence of God. I was bitter about a holiday presentation by the Campus Ministry team, when I would rather have been teaching my junior morality class. That's right. Our departments usually worked closely together, and I was complaining.

It was only my first year at the school. I had been teaching for the two previous years at a smaller school. I absolutely loved the students at my new school—kind, studious, open to me as a new teacher. But I thought that the school was too big. I missed my old school and my friends. Here we spent a lot of time in meetings. I also missed coaching sports. I didn't feel as involved as I wanted to be. By November, I was still skeptical about whether I would stay.

Campus Ministry's holiday presentation began. The lights dimmed and a large movie screen came down. "Earlier today . . ." flashed on the screen, and we were looking at a video from the side entrance of the school, an entrance that I did not use. There was a man who looked homeless, lost, and confused, and our students were talking to him. I saw a lot of kids I knew from my classes, whom I had seen around the hallway and as members of our sports teams. Then I saw my colleagues, those people in meetings at whom I had inwardly rolled my eyes; people who I saw in the hallways, who I shared rooms with; people who may not have known my name. Each person in the video offered the man something—money, a cellphone, coffee, clothing off their own backs. The most touching moment came when one of our parents left her car to give him her scarf. I choked down the lump in my throat as the screen went back up at the end of the video.

Suddenly, the same man appeared from a side door with one of my colleagues in Campus Ministry, and the room started to buzz with shock and surprise.

He walked up to the microphone, took it, and introduced himself. He was a De La Salle Christian Brother. He began to describe his work a few states away from us. We listened to him, and he told us many stories about how he, along with dedicated Lasallians like us, helped people make a better life for themselves.

As he talked, I kept thinking about all the work that went into bringing him to the school, and then keeping it a secret, so that the scene outside would be an authentic experience for our students. I replayed in my mind the genuine reactions of the people in the video, and how they knew instinctively that this man needed them, and how they went into action.

On that day, everything changed for me. I had come to the school looking for a charism that would most closely align with my values of living out the preferential option for the poor, standing in solidarity with others, and salvation through education. I had come looking for a closer encounter with the Incarnation. I had certainly found it.

Margaret Naughton
Lasallian Volunteers

Silence: Our Signature Prayer

Dictionaries tell us that a "signature" (/ˈsɪɡnətʃər/; from Latin: *signare,* "to sign") is a handwritten and often stylized depiction of someone's name, nickname, or even a simple "X" or other mark that a person writes on documents as a proof of identity and intent. By extension, we can talk about "signature" realities that belong to the identity of a person, place, thing, or idea.

In a recent religion class I asked our younger students what the "signature" mascot of Saint Paul's School is. They answered correctly that it is the wolf. I asked them what the "signature" colors of Saint Paul's School were, and again they answered correctly, affirming that the colors were blue and gold.

Then I asked them what the "signature" prayer of Saint Paul's is as a Lasallian school. There was a bit of a flurry as several of our daily vocal prayers were offered in answer. To each of these I answered "no." Finally, one of the students said, "I know. It is 'Let us remember that we are in the holy presence of God.'" "No," I said. "That is not a prayer. It is an invitation." Then one student ventured a stab in the dark. "Is it the silence after the invitation?"

"Yes," I said. "The silence is our signature prayer, and it should last about a minute. Like the diamond in an engagement ring, it is the silence that is our treasure, our diamond. All the rest is setting!"

Silence is our "being with" God and one another. Like the great commandment taught by Jesus, it is the two-fold presence that through the ambience created by silence speaks louder than words and captures the mystery of being one with God and one another. The silence is a unitive reality that in its simplicity brings us together in brotherhood, sisterhood, purpose, and mission.

We need not "do" anything. We are simply "with." Like a loving couple who have grown old in their love, silence enriches without anything else.

In his book *Explanation of the Method of Interior Prayer*, De La Salle talks about interior silence and the prayer of simple attention. He says that as we pray with words and ritual, we slip from time to time into a graced moment in which not words or actions, but rather silence reigns. He tells us not to be afraid of this "because we seem to be doing nothing," for it is resting in the loving presence of God and one another that is the summit of prayer.

Silence is a pregnant reality that births and gives life. In *The Twelve Virtues of a Good Teacher*, we see silence as a teaching tool far more powerful than words. In *The Conduct of the Christian Schools*, we see silence as the hallmark of accompaniment in the school that creates community and strengthens the bonds of formation and learning.

Like Rublev's painting of the Trinity, it is the silence that marks the presence of God and calls us to deeper bonds, moving us past any divisions of age, nationality, ability, race, or religion.

There is a great wisdom in our "signature prayer." The invitation announced by the prayer leader over and over in our day calls us to a moment of focus and authenticity, identity and intent. It is this moment of remembering the presence that is Gospel. What wisdom De La Salle and the first teachers had in creating this and leaving it to subsequent Lasallian generations. What a wonderful tradition!

Brother Jeffrey L. Calligan, FSC
Saint Paul's School, Covington, LA

If you would like to submit a reflection
that is similar to the ones in this
book for a future volume of this
publication, please email
communications@lasallian.info to learn more.